# ELM TREE BOOKS

# TIME-TESTED COOKBOOK

| | |
|---|---|
| Cookery Editor | Mary Pope |
| Sub-Editor | Jennifer Stevenson |
| Design | Bryan Austin Associates |

First published in 1970 by LIVING
Elm House
Elm Street
LONDON WC1X 0BP

Revised Edition 1979

© 1979 Standbrook Publications Ltd.
a member of the Thomson Organisation Ltd.

Distributed to the book trade by
Elm Tree Books/Hamish Hamilton Ltd,
Garden House, 57/59 Long Acre, London
WC2E 9JZ

ISBN 0 241 10391 6

Printed by Sackville Press Billericay Ltd.

# CONTENTS

HOW TO USE THE CLOCKS

Above each recipe you'll see two clocks like this. The black clock gives you the approximate number of minutes' preparation time (time you'll spend in the kitchen). The white clock gives you the number of minutes' cooking or setting time (when you may be free to leave the kitchen). Add them together before you start cooking and you will have an idea how long each recipe will take.

*In this book a teaspoon is equal to a 5 ml spoon, and a tablespoon is 15 ml. All ingredients are given in both metric and imperial measurements, but it is important that you follow either metric or imperial figures in any one recipe.*

**Cover picture:**
Sweet- sour
Barbecue Kebabs

# INTRODUCTION

Our time-tested recipes have long been a successful feature in Living magazine, and our first Time-Tested Cookbook was an instant success. So to launch a new series of cookery books we decided to reprint this old favourite. We've given it a completely new look. The text has been updated, we've added more than 30 new recipes from our files, and most importantly, we give the quantities in both metric and imperial measures.

Mary Pope,
Cookery Editor

**Italian-style Chicken,** see opposite page

# MEAT

*The traditional basis of a main family meal, meat is an important source of protein, vitamin B and iron. These time-tested recipes help busy cooks experiment with new recipes–from a 20-minute family curry to a dinner-party gammon joint*

## LEMON AND HONEY CHICKEN

*(Serves 4)*
50 g (2oz) butter
4 chicken joints, trimmed if necessary
juice of 1 lemon
4 level tablespoons clear honey
freshly ground black pepper
fresh rosemary, chopped (optional)
parsley and lemon wedges to garnish

1 Heat the butter in a medium-sized frying pan with a lid (or use a sheet of kitchen foil to cover).
2 Place the chicken joints in the pan and brown them lightly all over.
3 Cover and cook slowly for 25 minutes, turning once.
4 When the chicken is cooked add the lemon juice, honey, black pepper and rosemary (if used).
5 Raise the heat and baste the chicken with the mixture until it thickens slightly—about 2 minutes.
6 Place the chicken on a hot serving dish and spoon the liquor over. Sprinkle with a little chopped parsley, and garnish with lemon wedges.

## ITALIAN-STYLE CHICKEN

*(Serves 4)*
4 chicken joints, fully thawed if frozen
juice of 1 lemon
salt and pepper
50 g (2oz) butter
2 slices ham or 4 bacon rashers
4 thin slices Bel Paese or Edam cheese
175-225 g (6-8oz) egg noodles
1 tablespoon chopped parsley to garnish

1 Preheat a moderately hot oven (190 deg C, 375 deg F, Gas 5), centre shelf.
2 Place the chicken in a small roasting tin, squeeze the lemon juice over, season well and dot with butter.
3 Roast chicken in the oven for 30 minutes, basting occasionally with the juices in the tin.
4 Remove chicken from the oven, and place half a piece of ham or a rasher of bacon on each joint. Cover it with a slice of cheese and return to the oven for 10 minutes.
5 Meanwhile, cook the egg noodles in a saucepan of boiling water for 5-8 minutes, or according to the instructions on the packet.
6 Drain the noodles well. Pour on any butter and juice from the roasting tin and toss well to coat.
7 Arrange noodles on a warmed serving dish, sprinkle with parsley and place chicken joints on top.
Note: If necessary, grill the chicken for 2 minutes to brown it.
*See picture opposite*

7

## ROAST CHICKEN WITH APRICOT STUFFING

*(Serves 8)*
2½ kg (6lb) chicken or capon
¼ lemon
50 g (2oz) butter
salt and pepper
3 rashers streaky bacon
APRICOT STUFFING
125 g (4oz) dried apricots, soaked overnight in cold water
125 g (4oz) fresh white breadcrumbs
¼ level teaspoon mixed spice
salt and pepper
1 tablespoon lemon juice
25 g (1oz) butter
1 egg, beaten

**1** Preheat a moderately hot oven (190 deg C, 375 deg F, Gas 5), centre shelf.
**2 To make the stuffing:** Drain the apricots and chop into small pieces. Place in a mixing bowl. Add the bread-crumbs, spice, seasoning and lemon juice. Melt the butter and add to the bowl with the egg. Mix well.
**3** Press the stuffing into the neck end of the bird under the flap of skin, taking care to give the breast a nice plump shape. Secure the flap of skin with a safety pin or skewer.
**4** Place the ¼ lemon inside the body cavity, rub the butter over the chicken and sprinkle with salt and pepper.
**5** Put the chicken in a roasting tin and cover with bacon rashers.
**6** Roast in oven until tender—about 1½ hours, basting frequently. Fifteen minutes before the end of cooking, remove the bacon to brown the breast.
**7** Keep chicken hot on a serving dish while you make gravy in the usual way.

## MEAT LOAF IN BACON

*(Serves 4)*
75 g (3oz) white bread, without crusts
4 tablespoons milk
450 g (1lb) minced beef
1 onion, finely chopped
1 level tablespoon chopped parsley
1 teaspoon Worcestershire sauce
salt and pepper
2 eggs, lightly beaten
4 rashers streaky bacon, trimmed

**1** Preheat a moderately hot oven (190 deg C, 375 deg F, Gas 5). Grease a 450 g (1lb) loaf tin or a small cake tin.
**2** Place the bread in a small bowl and pour the milk over. Press down and leave to soak.
**3** Place the minced beef in a mixing bowl, and add the onion, parsley, Worcestershire sauce and seasoning.
**4** Mash the bread with a fork until fine. Add to the meat mixture, then stir in the eggs and work all ingredients well together.
**5** 'Spread' the rashers with the back of a knife and arrange in the tin to cover most of the base and sides.
**6** Press the meat mixture into the tin and smooth the surface. Cover tin with greased foil and place on a small baking tin.
**7** Cook the loaf in the oven for 1 hour. The loaf is cooked if juices come out clear when a thin, sharp knife is inserted in the centre.
**8** Turn out on to a heated serving dish and cut into slices.
*See picture on page 10*

## MARMALADE GLAZED GAMMON

*(Serves 10)*
2¼-2¾ kg (5-6lb) gammon hock, soaked
  overnight in cold water
1.65 litres (3 pints) water
a few onions and carrots, peeled
cloves
350 g (12oz) chunky marmalade
orange slices and watercress to garnish

**1** Drain and weigh gammon joint and calculate cooking time, allowing 20 minutes per 450 g (1lb) plus 20 minutes' extra cooking time.
**2** Place the gammon in a large saucepan, cover with fresh water, and add onions and carrots.
**3** Cover and bring to the boil, then reduce the heat and simmer for required cooking time.
**4** When time is up, leave the joint to cool slightly before lifting it from the saucepan. Keep the liquid that it has cooked in but discard all the vegetables.
**5** Preheat a hot oven (220 deg C, 425 deg F, Gas 7), centre shelf.
**6** Carefully strip skin from the joint using a small sharp knife to loosen it from the fat, and place the joint in a roasting tin.
**7** Score the fat in a diagonal pattern with the knife, press a clove into each diamond shape, and cover the fat with the marmalade.
**8** Pour 150 ml (¼ pint) ham liquid into the roasting tin.
**9** Bake in the oven for 30 minutes, basting once with any marmalade that slides off as it cooks.
**10** Drain from the stock and arrange the joint on a heated serving dish. Garnish with orange slices and sprigs of watercress.

*See picture on page 11*

## HAM AND MUSHROOM VOL-AU-VENTS

*(Serves 4)*
**4 large individual vol-au-vent cases**
**75 g (3 oz) butter or margarine**
**1 medium-sized onion, chopped**
**125 g (4oz) mushrooms, thinly sliced**
**50 g (2oz) plain flour**
**400 ml (¾ pint) milk**
**125 g (4oz) ham, diced**
**salt and pepper**
**sprigs of parsley to garnish**

**1** Preheat a moderately hot oven (190 deg C, 375 deg F, Gas 5), centre shelf.
**2** Place the vol-au-vent cases on a baking sheet (remove their pastry lids if they have them) and heat through in the oven for about 10 minutes, while preparing the filling.
**3** Melt the butter or margarine in a small saucepan and add the onion. Cook gently without browning until soft—about 10 minutes.
**4** Add the mushrooms to the saucepan and cook for 3 minutes.
**5** Then stir in the flour and cook for 3 minutes, stirring occasionally. Gradually blend in the milk and bring to the boil, stirring. Simmer for 2 minutes, then add the ham to the sauce and heat through gently. Add salt and pepper to taste.
**6** Arrange vol-au-vent cases on a warmed serving dish and spoon the sauce into them. Serve any extra sauce in a sauce boat. Replace pastry lids, and garnish the dish with parsley sprigs. Serve at once.

## SIMPLE RISOTTO

*(Serves 3-4)*
**25 g (1oz) butter or margarine**
**1 medium-sized onion, coarsely chopped**
**2 sticks celery, thinly sliced**
**2 gammon steaks**
**50 g (2oz) mushrooms, chopped**
**175 g (6oz) long-grain rice**
**400 ml (¾ pint) chicken stock, or water and stock cube**
**50 g (2oz) frozen peas**
**salt and pepper**

**1** Melt the butter or margarine in a large frying pan. Add the onion and celery and cook slowly without browning until soft—about 10 minutes.

**2** Remove any surplus fat from the gammon steaks and cut them into strips 1 by 4 cm (½ by 1½in).
**3** Add the gammon and mushrooms to the pan and cook for 5 minutes.
**4** Add the rice to the pan, stir and cook for 2 minutes.
**5** Add most of the stock, bring to the boil and cook gently till rice is tender and liquid has been absorbed—about 25 minutes. Pour in the remaining stock, if required. Five minutes before the end of the cooking time, add the frozen peas.
**6** Season with salt and pepper. Serve at once.

## OVEN-BAKED SPARE RIBS

*(Serves 4)*
**2 tablespoons oil**
**4 spare rib pork chops**
**1 medium-sized onion, chopped**
**2 level tablespoons sweet pickle**
**250 ml (½ pint) pineapple juice**
**1 tablespoon soy sauce**
**1 tablespoon wine vinegar**
**a few drops Worcestershire sauce**
**2 level tablespoons demerara sugar**
**2 level tablespoons cornflour**
**3 tablespoons water**
**salt and pepper**

**1** Preheat a moderate oven (180 deg C, 350 deg F, Gas 4), centre shelf.
**2** Heat the oil in a frying pan and lightly brown the chops on both sides. Remove with a draining spoon into an ovenproof dish.
**3** Cook the onion in the frying pan until soft but not brown, and add the pickle, pineapple juice, soy sauce, vinegar, Worcestershire sauce and sugar.
**4** Blend the cornflour with the water till smooth. Add to the sauce, stirring until thickened. Simmer for 2 minutes and season to taste.
**5** Pour the sauce over the chops, cover, and cook in the oven for 1 hour. Serve very hot.

**Meat Loaf in Bacon,** see page 8

**Marmalade Glazed Gammon,** see page 8

11

## PORK AND VEAL LOAF

*(Serves 4-6)*
225 g (8oz) veal, minced
225 g (8oz) pork, minced
225 g (8oz) streaky bacon, trimmed and minced
125 g (4oz) fresh white breadcrumbs
1 medium-sized onion, finely chopped
2 large oranges
2 eggs, beaten
1 level teaspoon dried mixed herbs
salt and pepper
3 level tablespoons demerara sugar
2 level teaspoons arrowroot
orange slices and watercress to garnish

1 Preheat a warm oven (170 deg C, 325 deg F, Gas 3), centre shelf. Grease a 450 g (1lb) loaf tin.
2 Mix the minced meats together in a bowl , add the breadcrumbs, onion, the grated rind of one orange, the eggs, herbs and seasoning. Mix all the ingredients well together.
3 Pack mixture into the loaf tin, cover with foil, place in a baking tin half filled with water, and bake in the oven for 1½ hours.
4 When loaf is cooked, remove from the tin and place on a heated serving dish. Keep hot.
5 Meanwhile, squeeze the juice from the two oranges and put into a small saucepan with the sugar. Heat to allow sugar to dissolve, stirring if necessary. Bring to the boil and continue boiling for 2 minutes. Blend the arrowroot with a little water and stir into the orange juice. Continue stirring until mixture thickens; bring to the boil and simmer until clear.
6 Remove from heat and pour sauce over the loaf. Decorate with small sprigs of watercress and extra slices of orange, if liked.

## GINGERED ROAST PORK

*(Serves 10)*
2¾ kg (6lb) leg of pork
1 level tablespoon ground ginger
salt and pepper
1 level teaspoon dried mixed herbs
1 tablespoon oil
2 level tablespoons clear honey

1 A few hours before cooking rub the joint with the ground ginger, seasoning and herbs, and brush with oil.

Sprinkle a little extra ground ginger in the roasting tin and place the joint on top. Leave for at least 2 hours in a cool place.
2 To roast joint, preheat a moderately hot oven (190 deg C, 375 deg F, Gas 5), centre shelf.
3 Rub the honey over the joint. Roast the meat in the oven for 3½ hours, basting occasionally.
4 Remove the cooked meat to a heated serving dish and keep warm.
5 Pour off the fat and make gravy in the usual way, adding a little extra ginger, if liked.

## VEAL POLPETTE

*(Serves 4)*
**TOMATO SAUCE**
400 g (14oz) can tomatoes
1 small onion, roughly chopped
1 bay leaf
salt and pepper
1 level teaspoon sugar
1 tablespoon oil
**VEAL MEATBALLS**
40 g (1½oz) stale white bread, no crusts
5 tablespoons milk
1 medium-sized onion, grated or finely chopped
1 level tablespoon chopped parsley
600 g (1¼lb) veal, minced,
salt and pepper
¼ level teaspoon dried thyme
grated rind of ½ lemon
1 tablespoon plain flour
oil for frying
bay leaves to garnish

1 **To make the tomato sauce:** Place all the ingredients in a small saucepan and bring to the boil.
2 Simmer uncovered for 20 minutes, stirring sauce occasionally with a wooden spoon to break up tomatoes. Then boil quickly for 5 minutes to reduce to a thick consistency.
3 Remove the bay leaf, sieve the sauce, and return mixture to pan. Adjust seasoning to taste and place the pan on one side.
4 **To make the meatballs:** Crumble the bread into a mixing bowl. Pour the milk over and press down with a fork. Leave to soak.
5 Add the onion, parsley, veal, seasoning, thyme and lemon rind to the bread and mix well.
6 Flour hands lightly and form the mixture into small balls about 2.5 cm (1in) in diameter. Toss these gently in flour.
7 Heat just enough oil to cover the base of a frying pan and carefully lower in the meatballs. Fry gently for 10-15 minutes, turning so that all sides are evenly browned. Take care to turn them gently so that the meatballs do not break up. Meanwhile reheat the sauce.
8 Pile meatballs on a hot plate and garnish with a couple of bay leaves. Serve with the tomato sauce.

## BREAST OF LAMB SUPERB

*(Serves 4)*
2 tablespoons cooking oil
salt and pepper
1 kg (2lb) stuffed breast of lamb
6 level tablespoons redcurrant jelly
2 level tablespoons clear honey
4 small gherkins, chopped
2 tablespoons wine vinegar
watercress and potato crisps (optional) to garnish

1 Preheat a moderate oven (180 deg C, 350 deg F, Gas 4), shelf above centre.
2 Heat a little oil in a roasting tin. Season lamb and place in the roasting tin and baste with the oil. Roast in the oven for 1½ hours.
3 When cooked, remove string, cut into thick slices and arrange on a heated serving dish. Keep hot.
4 Measure the redcurrant jelly and honey into a small saucepan, heat gently until melted. Add the gherkins and wine vinegar, mix well and heat through.
5 Pour the sauce over the lamb. Garnish with the watercress and potato crisps, if liked.

## QUICK LAMB CURRY

*(Serves 2-3)*
125 g (4oz) long-grain rice
298 g (10½oz) can mulligatawny soup
1 rounded teaspoon curry paste
1 tablespoon chutney
1 rounded tablespoon sultanas
350 g (12oz) cooked lamb, diced

1 Bring a saucepan of salted water to the boil. Add the rice, stir well and cook for about 12 minutes or until just tender. Then drain, rinse and keep hot.
2 Meanwhile pour the soup into a small saucepan. Add the curry paste, chutney and sultanas, and heat gently until steaming.
3 Stir the meat into the curry sauce and heat through gently for about 5 minutes.
4 Arrange the rice round the edge of a heated serving dish and pour the curry into the centre. Serve at once.

## CROWN ROAST OF LAMB

*(Serves 6)*
1 crown of lamb (12-14 bones) (order in advance and ask the butcher to keep the meat trimmings separately)
1 medium-sized onion, quartered
1 medium-sized cooking apple, peeled, cored and quartered
25 g (1oz) walnut pieces
40 g (1½oz) fresh white breadcrumbs
1 level teaspoon dried thyme
salt and pepper
1 kg (2lb) potatoes, peeled and cut to even-sized pieces for roasting
fat or dripping for roasting
paper cutlet frills (optional)
watercress or orange slices to garnish

1 Preheat a moderately hot oven (190 deg C, 375 deg F, Gas 5), centre shelf.
2 Remove surplus fat from the meat trimmings, mince the trimmed meat with the onion, apple and walnuts into a mixing bowl.
3 Add the breadcrumbs, thyme and seasoning. Mix well.
4 Stuff the centre of the crown, pressing the stuffing down well. Cover end of each bone with a piece of foil.
5 Weigh the crown and calculate cooking time, allowing 20 minutes per 450 g (1lb) and 20 minutes over. Place the crown in a roasting tin.
6 Place potatoes round the joint. Dot with fat or dripping.
7 Roast the joint in the hot oven for the calculated time. Turn the potatoes occasionally.
8 When cooked, remove the crown from the oven and arrange on a hot serving dish. Put potatoes in a hot vegetable dish. Remove the foil from the bones and replace with cutlet frills, if using. Keep hot while making gravy in the usual way.
9 Garnish with watercress and slices of orange. Serve potatoes separately.

*See picture on next page*

## LAMB CHOPS PRINCESS

*(Serves 4)*
**1 egg**
**2 teaspoons water**
**75 g (3oz) bread sauce mix**
**8 best end of neck chops**
**50 g (2oz) butter or margarine**
**25 g (1oz) plain flour**
**298 g (10½oz) can beef consommé**
**1 tablespoon red wine vinegar**
**4 small gherkins, sliced.**

**1** Break the egg on to a dish, add the water and beat well with a fork.
**2** Put the bread sauce mix on to another plate.
**3** Dip a chop into the egg, drain a little and then coat with bread sauce mix. Repeat for remaining 7 chops.
**4** Heat the butter or margarine in a large frying pan, place the chops in the pan and cook gently for 15 minutes, turning once.
**5** Remove the chops and arrange them overlapping along the centre of a heated serving dish and keep hot.
**6** Stir the flour into the remaining butter in the pan and cook for 2 minutes.
**7** Blend in the consommé, stirring continuously, add the wine vinegar and cook for 3 minutes.
**8** Add gherkins to the sauce and spoon over the chops.

## FLEMISH STEW

*(Serves 6)*
**1 kg (2lb) chuck steak**
**3 tablespoons dripping**
**125 g (4oz) onions, sliced**
**1 level tablespoon demerara sugar**
**1 clove crushed garlic (optional)**
**25 g (1oz) plain flour**
**250 ml (½ pint) brown ale**
**250 ml (½ pint) beef stock, or water and stock cube**
**1 bay leaf**
**1 tablespoon wine vinegar**
**20 cm (8in) length French bread**
**French mustard**

**1** Preheat a warm oven (170 deg C, 325 deg F, Gas 3), centre shelf.
**2** Trim the meat and cut into 4 cm (1½in) cubes. Melt the dripping in a large saucepan and quickly brown the meat on all sides. Lift meat into a large ovenproof casserole.
**3** Add the onions to the dripping in the saucepan and

Crown Roast of Lamb, see page 13

cook until brown. Then add the sugar, crushed garlic (if using) and flour. Cook slowly for 2 minutes, stirring continuously to prevent sticking.

4 Blend in the brown ale and stock, or water and stock cube, then pour into casserole. Add bay leaf and vinegar to the gravy.

5 Cover and cook in the oven for 2-2½ hours, until the meat is tender.

6 Meanwhile cut the French bread into 1 cm (½in) rounds and on one side spread generously with French mustard, or to taste.

7 Remove casserole from oven, skim off any excess fat, and arrange the French bread on top of the stew, dunking it in the gravy a little. Leave casserole uncovered and replace it in the oven.

8 Cook for further 20-30 minutes until bread is brown and slightly crisp. Serve at once.

# OXTAIL HOT POT

(Serves 4)

2 small oxtails, jointed and soaked in cold water for at
  least 3 hours, or overnight
25 g (1oz) dripping
2 onions, sliced
1 carrot, sliced
1 rasher streaky bacon, trimmed and chopped
about 25 g (1oz) plain flour
1.15 litres (2 pints) beef stock, or water and 2 stock cubes
2 bay leaves
salt and pepper
6 peppercorns
a little cornflour

1 Drain the oxtails, then place in fresh cold water and bring to the boil. Skim the surface, and simmer for 10 minutes. Then drain the oxtails and dry thoroughly with kitchen paper.

2 Melt the dripping in a heavy saucepan and fry oxtails until lightly browned. Remove with a draining spoon and put on a plate.

3 Put the prepared vegetables and bacon in the saucepan and lightly brown. Pour off most of the fat and sprinkle in enough of the flour to absorb the fat which remains, without making it too dry or sticky.

4 Using a wooden spoon, gradually blend in the stock, or water and stock cubes. Replace the oxtail, add bay leaves, seasoning and peppercorns, and bring to the boil.

5 Cover well and simmer gently for about 3 hours, until meat falls easily away from the bones.

6 To serve, lift the meat into a large, hot serving dish and keep hot. Strain the gravy into a small pan and reduce by boiling rapidly. If necessary thicken with a little cornflour blended with water.

7 When reduced and thickened, pour over the oxtail and serve hot.

# CHUCK STEAK STROGANOFF

(Serves 6)

1 kg (2lb) chuck steak
50 g (2oz) plain flour, seasoned
2 tablespoons oil
1 medium-sized onion, coarsely chopped
298 g (10½oz) can condensed mushroom soup
1 rounded tablespoon tomato purée
150 g (5fl oz) natural yogurt
salt and pepper

1 Preheat a cool oven (150 deg C, 300 deg F, Gas 2), centre shelf.

2 Trim meat, removing skin and excess fat, and cut into strips. Toss in the seasoned flour, making sure it is well coated.

3 Heat the oil in a flameproof casserole or frying pan. Add the meat and fry until lightly browned—about 5 minutes.

4 Stir in the onion, soup, tomato purée and yogurt, and season to taste.

5 If using a frying pan, transfer its contents to a casserole, cover and cook in the oven for about 1½ hours until the meat is tender.

6 Serve hot with boiled rice.

# BEEFBURGER PASTIES

(Serves 2-4)

about 225 g (8oz) ready-made puff pastry
227 g (8oz) packet beefburgers
2 level tablespoons horseradish sauce
a little beaten egg to glaze

1 Preheat a hot oven (220 deg C, 425 deg F, Gas 7), shelf above centre.

2 Roll out the pastry on a lightly floured surface until large enough to give eight 13 cm (5in) diameter circles, using a saucer as a guide.

3 Place the beefburgers on 4 rounds of the pastry and spread them with horseradish sauce.

4 Brush the edges of the pastry with a little water and cover each with another circle of pastry. Press the edges together well to seal and flake up with the back of a knife. Flute the edges.

5 Place the pasties on a baking sheet, and brush lightly with egg to glaze.

6 Bake in the oven for 20-50 minutes until the pastry is golden brown.

7 Serve hot or cold with a green salad.

## CHICKEN LIVERS IN SOUR CREAM

*(Serves 4)*
**2 rashers streaky bacon**
**25 g (1oz) butter or margarine**
**1 small onion, finely chopped**
**500 g (1¼lb) chicken livers**
**½ level teaspoon dried sage**
**salt and pepper**
**150 ml (5fl oz) soured cream**
**225 g (8oz) long-grain rice**
**chopped parsley to garnish**

1 Trim off and keep the rinds and finely chop the bacon rashers.
2 Melt the butter in a frying pan and add the onions, bacon and bacon rinds. Cook gently, stirring occasionally, for 5 minutes
3 Trim the chicken livers and cut off any pieces of sinew or fat.
4 Remove the bacon rinds from the pan and discard. Add the livers and sage to the frying pan. Season well and cook gently for about 8 minutes, stirring occasionally.
5 Add the soured cream to the pan and mix well with the other ingredients. Simmer gently for a further 3 minutes.
6 Meanwhile, bring a large pan of salted water to the boil, add rice and cook for about 12 minutes, until tender. Drain and rinse with boiling water. Drain well.
7 Arrange cooked rice round the edge of a heated dish and pour the chicken livers into the centre. Sprinkle with parsley and serve hot.

## SAVOURY LIVER WITH APPLE

*(Serves 4)*
**8 rashers streaky bacon, trimmed**
**450 g (1lb) lambs' liver, sliced**
**2 level tablespoons plain flour, seasoned**
**250 ml (½ pint) beef stock, or water and stock cube**
**salt and pepper**
**1 medium-sized cooking apple**
**15 g (½oz) butter or margarine**
**sprigs of parsley to garnish**

1 Place the bacon rashers in a frying pan and cook gently, adding a little extra fat if necessary. When cooked, drain the bacon from the fat and keep hot.
2 Meanwhile, coat the liver in the seasoned flour, shaking off the excess.
3 Add the liver to the frying pan and cook in the bacon fat for about 7 minutes, turning once during cooking. Then

remove the liver from the pan and keep it hot.
4 Add the remaining seasoned flour to the pan and cook for 1 minute, stirring. Gradually blend in the stock and seasoning. Bring to the boil and simmer for 5 minutes. Pour into a sauce boat and keep hot.
5 Peel and core the apple and cut into 1 cm (½in) rings.
6 Clean the frying pan. Heat the butter or margarine and add the apple rings. Fry gently for about 2 minutes, turning once.
7 Arrange the liver on a serving dish with the apple and bacon. Pour a little sauce over and serve the rest separately. Garnish with parsley and serve hot.

## HOT TONGUE DIABLE

*(Serves 4)*
**4 slices cold cooked tongue**
**3 level tablespoons French mustard**
**¼ level tablespoon cayenne pepper**
**6 level tablespoons dried breadcrumbs**
**50 g (2oz) butter**

1 Place the tongue on a board, spread a little mustard over both sides of the tongue slices, and sprinkle with the cayenne pepper.
2 Coat with breadcrumbs, pressing the crumbs on both sides so the slices are well coated.
3 Preheat a moderately hot grill, place the slices on a grill rack and dot with butter.
4 Grill the tongue slices, turning once, until they are heated through and the crumbs are a golden brown.

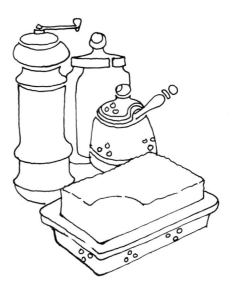

17

**Beefburgers Hawaii,** see page 20

**Spicy Baked Pork Chops,** see page 21

# BEEFBURGERS HAWAII

*(Serves 4)*
**227 g (8oz) can sliced pineapple**
**2 level tablespoons demerara sugar**
**2 tablespoons soy sauce**
**1 tablespoon wine vinegar**
**salt and pepper**
**1 level tablespoon cornflour**
**1 tablespoon capers, chopped**
**oil or fat for frying**
**two 226 g (8oz) packets frozen beefburgers**
**4 slices white bread**
**watercress to garnish**

**1** Drain pineapple and make juice up to 150 ml (¼ pint) with water. Place in saucepan with sugar, soy sauce, vinegar and seasoning. Heat to dissolve sugar. Blend cornflour with 2 tablespoons water and stir into pan, bring to boil, stirring, and cook until it thickens and clears. Add capers, and keep sauce hot.
**2** Fry or grill beefburgers as directed. Keep hot.
**3** Trim bread into 4 squares a little larger than the beefburgers. Fry in oil or fat, turning once, until crisp and golden on both sides, drain on kitchen paper. Fry pineapple rings quickly to heat.
**4** Arrange fried bread on a heated dish. Top each piece with 2 beefburgers, 1 pineapple slice, and sauce to glaze. Garnish with watercress and serve at once.

*See picture on page 18*

# AUTUMN CASSEROLE

*(Serves 4)*
**4 rabbit joints**
**plain flour, seasoned, to coat**
**50 g (2oz) butter or margarine**
**1 medium-sized onion, sliced**
**225 g (8oz) cooking apples, peeled, cored**
 **and cut into thick slices**
**227 g (8oz) can prunes**
**1 chicken stock cube**
**15 g (½oz) butter**
**15 g (½oz) plain flour**
**salt and pepper**
**chopped parsley and triangles of fried bread to garnish**

**1** Preheat a moderate oven (180 deg C, 350 deg F, Gas 4), centre shelf
**2** Coat rabbit joints in seasoned flour.
**3** Melt 50 g (2oz) butter or margarine in a flameproof casserole or frying pan. Add joints, lightly brown on all sides—about 5 minutes. Drain the joints and remove on to a plate.
**4** Add the onion and cook for 3 minutes, mix in the apples and toss lightly in the butter.
**5** Drain the prunes, reserve the liquor and make up to 250 ml (½ pint) with water and stock cube.
**6** Return the rabbit and add prunes to the casserole or, if you are using a frying pan, place prunes and rabbit with onion and apple in a clean casserole.
**7** Pour on the stock, cover and place in the oven. Cook for 1¼-1½ hours, until rabbit is tender—this can vary according to the type of rabbit.
**8** To serve, remove the rabbit, prunes, apples and onion and arrange on a preheated serving dish and keep hot while thickening the sauce.
**9** Blend the 15 g (½oz) each of butter and flour together with a knife on a plate. Add in small pieces to liquor in casserole, stirring, and bring to the boil stirring continuously until the sauce thickens.
**10** Season sauce to taste and pour over the rabbit. Sprinkle with chopped parsley and garnish with fried bread triangles. Serve at once.

# PORK AND APPLE PIE

*(Serves 4)*
**1 medium-sized onion, finely chopped**
**125 g (4oz) cooking apple,**
 **peeled, cored and finely chopped**
**350 g (12 oz) pork sausagemeat**
**1 level teaspoon dried mixed herbs**
**salt and pepper**
**397 g (14oz) packed frozen shortcrust**
 **pastry thawed**
**a little beaten egg**

**1** Preheat a moderately hot oven (200 deg C, 400 deg F, Gas 6), centre shelf.
**2** In a large bowl, mix together the onion, apple, sausagemeat, herbs and seasoning.
**3** Divide the pastry, not quite in half. Roll out the larger piece on a lightly floured surface and use to line an 18 cm (7in) shallow square tin.
**4** Arrange the filling evenly on the pastry.
**5** Roll out the remaining piece of pastry to fit over the top of the pie.
**6** Lightly damp the edges of the pastry in the tin and cover with the second piece of pastry. Seal the edges and trim the pie; crimp the edges with fingers. Brush the surface with the beaten egg.
**7** Bake in the oven for 15 minutes, then reduce temperature to moderate (180 deg C, 350 deg F, Gas 4) for a further 25 minutes, until the crust is golden brown and the filling is cooked.
**8** Serve either hot with cooked spring greens or cabbage or cold with a mixed salad.

## SPICY BAKED PORK CHOPS

*(Serves 4)*
1 kg (2lb) spare rib pork chops
SAUCE
2 large onions, chopped
2 cloves garlic, crushed
2 tablespoons chilli sauce
150 ml (¼ pint) vegetable oil
juice of 1 large lemon
4 tablespoons wine vinegar
1 level tablespoon soft brown sugar
½ level teaspoon salt
1 level teaspoon dry mustard
few drops of tabasco sauce (optional)
1 bay leaf

1 Place all the sauce ingredients in a pan, bring to the boil and simmer 10 minutes.
2 Preheat a moderate oven (180 deg C, 350 deg F, Gas 4), centre shelf.
3 Place pork chops on a grill rack in a shallow baking tin. Brush well with the sauce and bake in the oven for 1 hour, basting frequently.
4 Serve with boiled rice and a green vegetable.

*See picture on page 19*

## SMOKED SAUSAGE AND POTATO BAKE

*(Serves 4)*
350 g (12oz) onions, sliced
700 g (1½lb) potatoes, thinly sliced
225 (8oz) smoked sausages, thinly sliced
salt and pepper
1 tablespoon fresh rosemary sprigs
150 ml (¼ pint) chicken stock
1 tablespoon grated Parmesan cheese

1 Preheat a moderate oven (180 deg C, 350 deg F, Gas 4), centre shelf.
2 Arrange a thin layer of onion slices in an ovenproof dish, cover with a layer of potato, followed by a layer of sausage, seasoning each layer with salt and pepper and a sprinkling of rosemary. End with a layer of potato slices on the top.
3 Pour the chicken stock over and cover the dish with a lid or foil. Cook for 2 hours. Then remove lid or foil and sprinkle cheese over top. Continue cooking uncovered till golden brown—about ½ hour.

## HEARTWARMING CASSEROLE

*(Serves 3-4)*
4 calves' hearts, soaked in lightly salted
    water for half an hour
25 g (1oz) butter
1 rasher streaky bacon, trimmed and chopped
1 small onion, chopped
1 small carrot, finely sliced
25 g (1oz) plain flour
250 ml (½ pint) beef stock, or water and stock cube
228 g (8oz) can tomatoes
1 level teaspoon tomato purée
1 bay leaf
salt and pepper
1 tablespoon sherry (optional)

1 Drain the hearts and place in a pan of cold water. Bring to the boil, then drain again.
2 Cut the hearts in half lengthwise and, with a pair of scissors, remove all the veins and arteries. Cut flesh into 1 cm (½in) slices.
3 Melt the butter in a saucepan, add the sliced hearts and lightly brown. Remove from pan with a draining spoon, place in an ovenproof dish and set aside. Do not discard the butter.
4 To make the sauce, add the bacon, onion and carrot to the butter and cook gently until the onion and carrot are lightly brown—about 5 minutes.
5 Add the flour and brown it slightly without burning. Gradually blend in the stock, stirring continuously, then add tomatoes and their liquid and tomato purée. Bring to the boil, add the bay leaf, season to taste and add sherry if using. Cover and simmer for 20 minutes.
6 Preheat a warm oven (170 deg C, 325 deg F, Gas 3), centre shelf.
7 Strain the sauce over the hearts, cover and place in the oven for 1 hour, or until the hearts are tender.
8 Serve hot with a green vegetable.

**Forest Brown Stew,** see page 24

**Chicken Liver Kebabs,** see page 24

## FOREST BROWN STEW

*(Serves 4-6)*
**1 kg (2lb) chuck steak**
**50 g (2oz) beef dripping or cooking fat**
**225 g (8oz) onions, chopped**
**225 g (8oz) carrots, sliced**
**125 g (4oz) celery, cut in chunks**
**2 level tablespoons plain flour**
**275 ml (9.68 fl oz) can brown ale**
**2 level teaspoons tomato purée**
**400 ml (¾ pint) beef stock, or water and stock cube**
**salt and pepper**
**125 g (4oz) prunes, soaked overnight, or pour boiling water over and allow to stand for 15 minutes**

1 Trim the meat and cut into quite large cubes.
2 Melt the dripping or cooking fat in a fairly large saucepan, add the meat and fry quickly to seal in the juices. Lift out the meat with a draining spoon and keep on a plate.
3 Add the onions to the pan and cook gently for 10 minutes, until beginning to brown.
4 Preheat a warm oven (170 deg C, 325 deg F, Gas 3), centre shelf.
5 Add carrots and celery to the onions and cook for 5 minutes, stirring occasionally.
6 Return the meat to the pan, stir in the flour and blend in the brown ale, tomato purée, stock and seasonings. Bring to the boil.
7 Drain the prunes and add to the stew. Pour into a large casserole. Cook gently for 3 hours until the meat is tender and cooked through.

*See picture on page 22*

## SAUSAGE BINGO

*(Serves 4)*
**50 g (2oz) butter or margarine**
**1 large onion, chopped**
**125 g (4oz) carrots, peeled and cut into matchstick lengths**
**700 g (1½lb) green cabbage, finely shredded**
**salt and pepper**
**450 g (1lb) pork or beef sausages**
**40 g (1½oz) sultanas**

1 Melt the butter or margarine in a large frying pan with a lid. Add the chopped onion and carrot to the pan and cook slowly without browning, stirring occasionally, for 10 minutes.
2 Add the cabbage to the pan, mix the ingredients

together, add the seasoning, cover and cook gently for 20 minutes, stirring occasionally.
3 Meanwhile, preheat a moderate grill.
4 Separate the sausages and place on the grill rack. Grill for 15 minutes, turning during cooking.
5 Remove sausages from the grill rack and drain on kitchen paper.
6 Add the sultanas to the cabbage, mixing well.
7 Place the cabbage mixture on a heated serving dish. Arrange the sausages along the centre and serve.

## CHICKEN LIVER KEBABS

*(Serves 4)*
**350 g (12oz) chicken livers**
**8 small rashers streaky bacon, trimmed**
**4 small tomatoes**
**1 large green pepper, deseeded and cut into chunks**
**4 bay leaves**
**salt and pepper**
**oil**
**SAVOURY BUTTERED RICE**
**50 g (2oz) butter**
**225 g (8oz) cooked rice**
**4 spring onions, chopped**
**25 g (1oz) walnuts, chopped**
**50 g (2oz) sultanas**

1 **To prepare the kebabs:** Trim the chicken livers of any sinews and pieces of fat. Place in a small bowl and cover with boiling water. Leave for 1 minute then drain.
2 'Spread' each bacon rasher with the back of a knife and cut in half. Wrap a piece of bacon around each of the chicken livers.
3 Wipe and halve the tomatoes.
4 Divide all the kebab ingredients into 4 even portions. Thread them on to 4 skewers and season well. (They may be covered and stored for several hours in a refrigerator before cooking.)
5 **To cook the rice:** Melt butter in a frying pan, add rice and heat through, stirring occasionally, for 5 minutes.
6 Add spring onions, walnuts and sultanas to the rice, season, and mix well.
7 Turn rice on to a heated serving dish and keep hot.
8 **To cook kebabs:** Brush the kebabs with oil and grill for 8-10 minutes, turning occasionally.
10 Serve the kebabs on the rice.

*See picture on page 23*

## CURRIED TRIPE

*(Serves 6)*
1¼ kg (3lb) tripe
50 g (2oz) butter
2 large onions, coarsely chopped
1 eating apple, peeled, cored and coarsely chopped
2 level tablespoons curry powder
50 g (2oz) plain flour
550 ml (1 pint) chicken stock, or water and a stock cube
lemon wedges and chopped parsley to garnish

1 Wash tripe and cut into 5 cm (2in) squares. Place in a large saucepan, cover with cold water, and bring to the boil. Cover and simmer gently until it is really tender—at least 1 hour.
2 Melt the butter in a saucepan, add the onions and apple and fry gently until soft but not brown.
3 Add the curry powder and cook gently for 2 minutes. Then stir in the flour and cook for a further 2 minutes.
4 Gradually blend in the stock, or water and stock cube. Bring to boil, cover and simmer gently for 25 minutes, stirring occasionally.
5 Drain the tripe well and add to the sauce; reheat if necessary.
6 Garnish with lemon wedges and chopped parsley.

## CHIPOLATA MEDLEY

*(Serves 4)*
450 g (1lb) string of chipolata sausages
25 g (1oz) cooking fat
1 large onion, sliced
3 lambs' kidneys
25 g (1oz) plain flour, seasoned
250 ml (½ pint) beef stock, or water and a stock cube
50 g (2oz) streaky bacon, trimmed and chopped
125 g (4oz) button mushrooms
2 level teaspoons tomato purée
150 g (5oz) frozen peas
chopped parsley to garnish

1 Twist chipolatas in half but keep in the string.
2 Melt the fat in a flameproof casserole or frying pan and fry the sausages slowly until golden brown, turning frequently—about 10 minutes. Remove from the pan and keep hot.
3 Add the onion to the fat and cook slowly until golden brown and tender.
4 Meanwhile skin and halve the kidneys, and remove the cores.

5 Toss the kidneys in the seasoned flour and add to the onions in the casserole with any remaining flour.
6 Allow the flour to brown slowly without burning, then gradually blend in the stock and bring to the boil.
7 Add the bacon and mushrooms to the kidney mixture.
8 Cut sausages, add to the casserole or pan with the tomato purée and season to taste. Cover and simmer for 15 minutes. Then add the peas, cover and simmer for a further 10 minutes.
9 Serve hot sprinkled with chopped parsley.

## SWEET-SOUR BARBECUE KEBABS

*(Serves 4)*
700 g piece of boned top leg of lamb
8 rashers of streaky bacon, trimmed
227 g (8oz) can pineapple rings
125 g (4oz) button mushrooms
1 green pepper
225 g (8oz) packet boil-in-the-bag rice
**BARBECUE SAUCE**
1 tablespoon oil
1 small onion, grated
1 tablespoon wine or cider vinegar
3 tablespoons syrup from the pineapple rings
3 tablespoons soy sauce
3 level tablespoons soft brown sugar

1 **To prepare the kebabs:** Trim the meat and cut into 2.5 cm (1in) cubes. Roll up bacon into rolls.
2 Drain the pineapple rings, reserving the syrup, and cut each ring into 4.
3 Trim mushroom stalks. Remove seeds and white pith from the pepper and cut into squares.
4 Thread all the kebab ingredients on to 8 medium or 4 long kebab skewers.
5 Preheat a moderately hot grill.
6 **To make the sauce:** Meanwhile combine all the sauce ingredients in a small saucepan. Bring to the boil and boil for 1 minute. Remove from heat.
7 Brush the kebabs well with the sauce, and place on the grill rack. Grill for 15 minutes, turning frequently and brushing with more sauce.
8 Meanwhile, cook the rice as directed and turn on to a hot serving dish.
9 Place the kebabs on top of the rice, and serve with any remaining sauce.

*See picture on front cover*

**Party Peppers,** see page 28

**Chicken in the Pan,** see page 29

## PARTY PEPPERS

*(Serves 4-6)*
**3 tablespoons oil**
**1 clove garlic, crushed**
**1 large onion, chopped**
**50 g (2oz) long-grain rice**
**700 g (1½lb) minced beef**
**396 g (14oz) can tomatoes**
**¼ level teaspoon ground nutmeg**
**2 level teaspoons dried mint**
**1 level tablespoon chopped parsley**
**salt and pepper**
**4 large or 6 medium-sized peppers**
**25-40 g (1-1½oz) grated cheese**

1 Heat the oil in a saucepan. Add the garlic and onion and cook till just tender—about 5 minutes. Add rice and cook gently for 1 minute.
2 Stir in the mince and cook gently, stirring occasionally, till meat is brown.
3 Stir in the tomatoes and their juice, nutmeg, mint, parsley and seasoning to taste. Bring to the boil, cover and simmer for 30 minutes, stirring occasionally.
4 Preheat a moderately hot oven (190 deg C, 375 deg F, Gas 5), shelf above centre.
5 Cut the tops from the peppers and scoop out seeds and pith. Chop the flesh cut from the tops of peppers and add to the mince 5 minutes before end of cooking.
6 Blanch the pepper cups in boiling salted water for 10 minutes. Drain well.
7 Put the pepper cups in an ovenproof dish and spoon in the hot meat filling. Sprinkle the cheese on top.
8 Bake for 30-35 minutes till the tops are lightly browned. Serve hot or cold.

*See picture on page 26*

## SAVOURY STUFFED ONIONS

*(Serves 4)*
**4 large Spanish onions**
**25 g (1oz) long-grain rice**
**25 g (1oz) butter**
**125 g (4oz) mushrooms, chopped**
**125 g (4oz) cooked beef or lamb, coarsely minced**
**½ level teaspoon mixed dried herbs**
**1 level tablespoon tomato purée**
**salt and pepper**
**25 g (1oz) soft brown sugar**
**150 ml (¼ pint) beef stock, or water and stock cube**

1 Trim the onions, being careful not to remove too much of the base roots as these help to keep the onions together when stuffing.
2 Bring a large pan of salted water to the boil. Put in onions, simmer gently for 1 hour, then drain well.
3 Meanwhile, cook the rice in boiling salted water for 12 minutes or until tender; drain and rinse under hot water to separate the grains.
4 With the handle of a teaspoon carefully lift out the centres of the onions, starting right in the centre as this should prevent the outer skin from splitting. Remove all but about three layers of onion. Put the onion 'shells' in an ovenproof dish.
5 Chop the removed onion centres. Melt the butter in a pan, add the chopped onion and mushrooms and cook for 2 minutes. Add the meat, herbs, tomato purée, seasoning and rice.
6 Preheat a moderately hot oven (190 deg. C, 375 deg F, Gas 5), centre shelf.
7 In a small pan, dissolve the sugar in the beef stock and boil rapidly to reduce by half.
8 Fill the onions with the meat mixture. Pour the reduced liquid over, cover and cook in oven for 20 minutes.
9 Serve hot with a salad or any meat dish.

## PORK CHOPS WITH TOMATO ONION SAUCE

*(Serves 2)*
**2 small pork chops**
**salt and pepper**
**2 level tablespoons sage and onion stuffing mix**
**21 g (¾oz) packet onion sauce mix**
**250 ml (½ pint) milk**
**1 large or 2 small tomatoes, skinned and deseeded**
**parsley, chopped, to garnish**

1 Preheat a moderate oven (190 deg C, 375 deg F, Gas 5), shelf towards the top.
2 Sprinkle the chops with salt and pepper. Make up stuffing mix as directed, and spread over the chops. Place on an ovenproof dish or plate and bake for 25-30 minutes till chops are cooked through.
3 Meanwhile, make up and cook the sauce mix, as directed. Roughly chop the tomato, add to the sauce and heat gently for 1 minute.
4 Arrange chops on a heated dish. Pour over a little of the sauce and sprinkle with parsley. Serve the remaining sauce separately.

## CHICKEN IN THE PAN

*(Serves 4-6)*
4-6 chicken joints
25 g (1oz) plain flour, seasoned
25 g (1oz) butter
1 onion, chopped
3 sticks celery, chopped
2 small green and/or red peppers, deseeded and diced
410 g (14½oz) can pineapple tidbits
400 ml (¾ pint) chicken stock
2 level teaspoons paprika
pinch dried thyme
175 g (6oz) cut macaroni or shell pasta

1 Preheat a moderate oven (180 deg C, 350 deg F, Gas 4), centre shelf.
2 Toss the chicken joints in the seasoned flour.
3 Heat the butter in a flameproof casserole and fry the chicken until brown all over. Drain joints and reserve.
4 Add the onion, celery and peppers to the fat remaining in casserole and cook gently 3-4 minutes. Sprinkle in any remaining flour and mix well.
5 Remove from heat and gradually blend in pineapple tidbits and juice, stock, paprika, thyme and pasta.
6 Return chicken joints to pan and cover with lid or foil.
7 Cook in oven about 60 minutes until chicken is tender.

*See picture on page 27*

## PROVENÇALE LAMB

### Pressure-cooked recipe
*(Serves 4)*
¾ kg (about 1½lb) neck of lamb
1 large onion, sliced
396 g (14oz) can peeled tomatoes
1 level teaspoon stock powder
2 cloves garlic, crushed
salt and pepper
scant 150 ml (¼ pint) water
350g (12oz) potatoes, sliced
chopped parsley to garnish

1 Wipe the meat and remove any small pieces of bone.
2 Place in the pressure cooker, arrange onion over the top, pour in the tomatoes, breaking up large ones. Sprinkle in the stock powder, garlic, salt and pepper. Add the water.
3 Cover and bring to High (15lb) pressure in the usual way and cook for 20 minutes, maintaining the pressure.

4 Reduce pressure, remove lid, cover surface with potatoes, season. Replace lid, bring back to pressure again and cook for a further 10 minutes. Reduce pressure.
5 Serve sprinkled with chopped parsley.
**Note:** It is very important to follow the manufacturer's instruction when using a pressure cooker.

## GAMMON WITH CHIVE AND CUCUMBER SAUCE

*(Serves 4)*
1 kg (2lb) piece gammon
1 small onion
1 small carrot
1 bay leaf (optional)
¼ cucumber, peeled and roughly diced
40 g (1½oz) butter or margarine
2 level tablespoons flour
250 ml (½ pint) milk
small bunch chives, chopped
pepper and salt

1 Soak gammon covered with cold water for 5-6 hours if possible. (If gammon is pre-packed, check label directions to see whether it needs to be soaked.)
2 Drain and weigh meat and place in a saucepan. Cover with fresh cold water, bring slowly to boil. If joint has not soaked very long, drain and bring to boil again in enough fresh water to cover.
3 Add onion, carrot and bay leaf (if using), cover and simmer, allowing 20 minutes per 450 g (1lb) plus 20 minutes over. Drain and strip off the skin.
4 Meanwhile cook cucumber in 15 g (½oz) fat until soft—5-10 minutes. Place in a dish and clean the pan.
5 Melt the remaining fat, stir in flour, cook gently. Blend in milk and bring to boil, stirring. Cook for 1 minute.
6 Stir in about 3 tablespoons of stock from the gammon to make a good pouring consistency and add the cucumber and chives. Season with pepper, taste and add salt if needed. Serve hot with the gammon.

*See picture on page 31*

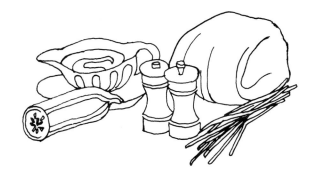

**Quick Beef Stew,** see page 32

**Gammon with Chive and Cucumber Sauce,** see page 29

## HOT BACON WITH
## SOMERSET SAUCE

*(Serves 6)*
**700 g (1½lb) picnic shoulder tendersweet bacon joint**
**17 g (10dr) packet white sauce mix**
**150 ml (¼ pint) milk**
**3 tablespoons cider**
**50 g (2oz) seedless raisins**
**1 dessert apple, cored and chopped**

**1** Roast or boil bacon joint as directed on wrapper, about 1-1¼ hours.
**2** Blend the sauce mix with milk until smooth, add the cider, raisins and apple. Bring to boil, stirring continuously and simmer for 1 minute. Add 2 tablespoons milk to thin consistency, if necessary.
**3** Serve the sauce with the hot sliced bacon and a salad.

## STEAK, KIDNEY
## AND MUSHROOM PIE

*(Serves 4)*
**450 g (1lb) stewing steak**
**125 g (4oz) ox kidney**
**25 g (1oz) butter**
**25 g (1oz) plain flour**
**250 ml (½ pint) red wine**
**1 teaspoon Worcestershire sauce**
**salt and pepper**
**125 g (4oz) mushrooms, quartered**
**1 tablespoon chopped parsley**
**212 g (7½oz) packet frozen puff pastry, thawed**
**beaten egg to glaze**

**1** Trim steak and kidney and cut into 2 cm (¾in) pieces. Heat the butter in a pan, add meats and fry till brown.
**2** Stir in the flour, then gradually blend in the wine, Worcestershire sauce and seasoning to taste. Bring to boil, cover and simmer for 1¾ hours.
**3** Then add the mushrooms and parsley and cook for a further 10 minutes. Turn into 825 ml (1½ pint) pie dish and allow to cool.
**4** Preheat a moderately hot oven (200 deg C, 400 deg F, Gas 6), shelf just above centre.
**5** Roll out the pastry on a lightly floured surface, to an oval about 2 cm (¾in) larger than the pie dish. Cut 1 cm (½in) strips of pastry from edge of the oval and press firmly on to dampened rim of pie dish.
**6** Damp this pastry edge and lift on the large piece of

pastry. Seal, trim and crimp the edges. Cut decorative pastry leaves from the trimmings.
**7** Brush pastry top with egg, arrange the leaves on top and brush with more egg.
**8** Place the pie on a baking tray and bake for 35-40 minutes till golden on top and well heated through. Serve hot.

## QUICK BEEF STEW

### Pressure-cooked recipe
*(Serves 4-5)*
**700 g (about 1½lb) chuck steak**
**25 g (1oz) beef dripping**
**125 g (4oz) button onions, peeled**
**1 small onion, chopped**
**2 carrots, sliced**
**1 beef stock cube**
**425 ml (¾ pint) boiling water**
**salt and pepper**
**1 level tablespoon flour**

**1** Trim and cut the meat into 2.5 cm (1in) cubes. Heat the dripping in the pressure cooker, add the meat, and fry until brown. Drain and remove from pan.
**2** Add the onions and carrots to the fat and cook till lightly brown. Return the meat to the pressure cooker with the beef cube dissolved in boiling water and season.
**3** Cover, bring to High (15lb) pressure in the usual way, cook for 30 minutes. Reduce pressure and remove lid.
**4** Blend the flour with a little water and then a little hot stock. Pour the mixture into the pan and bring to boil, stirring continuously. Cook for 1 minute, then transfer to a heated serving dish.
**Note:** It is very important to follow the manufacturer's instructions when using a pressure cooker.
*See picture on page 30*

## SUMMER BRAISED
## LAMB CHOPS

*(Serves 4)*
**2 tablespoons oil**
**4 lamb chump chops**
**1 medium-sized onion, sliced**
**1 large aubergine, sliced**
**4 sticks celery, sliced**
**450 g (1lb) tomatoes, quartered**
**½ level teaspoon chopped fresh rosemary, or ¼ level**
  **teaspoon dried rosemary**
**250 ml (½ pint) red wine**
**1 level teaspoon salt**
**black pepper**

1 Heat the oil in a frying pan and fry chops until browned on both sides. Drain and remove from the pan.
2 Fry the onion for 1 minute, then add the aubergine and celery and fry for 5 minutes over medium heat, stirring occasionally.
3 Stir in the tomatoes, rosemary, wine, salt and pepper. Place the chops on top, cover and simmer for 20 minutes until vegetables and meat are tender.
4 Serve hot straight from the pan.

# CHICKEN LASAGNE

*(Serves 2-3)*
1 tablespoon oil
125 g (4oz) lasagne
25 g (1oz) butter or margarine
1 medium-sized onion, chopped
2 cloves garlic, crushed (optional)
175 g (6oz) mushrooms, chopped
350 g (12oz) cooked chicken, boned and coarsely chopped
salt and pepper
1 tablespoon dry sherry (optional)
SAUCE
40 g (1½oz) butter or margarine
25 g (1oz) plain flour
400 ml (¾ pint) milk
175 g (6oz) Emmenthal cheese, grated
salt and pepper

1 Bring a large pan of salted water to boil. Add the oil and lasagne and cook as directed on the packet. Drain well in a colander.
2 Melt the butter or margarine in a medium-sized saucepan, add the onion and garlic, and cook until soft without browning—about 5 minutes. Then add the chopped mushrooms and cook gently for a further 5 minutes. Remove pan from the heat.
3 Add the chicken to the pan with the salt, pepper and sherry (if used). Mix well.
4 Preheat a moderate oven (180 deg C, 350 deg F, Gas 4), centre shelf. Butter a 20 cm (8in) square ovenproof dish.
5 **To make the sauce:** Melt the butter or margarine in a saucepan, add the flour and cook for 3 minutes without browning. Gradually blend in the milk, stirring continuously. Bring to the boil and simmer for 2 minutes, still stirring continuously.
6 Add all but 3 level tablespoons of the cheese to the sauce. Heat gently until the cheese is melted, and add salt and pepper to taste.
7 Line the base of the ovenproof dish with pieces of cooked lasagne. Cover it with alternate layers of chicken, sauce and lasagne, finishing with a layer of lasagne topped with the remaining cheese sauce. Sprinkle with the remaining grated cheese.
8 Heat in oven 30 minutes until top is lightly browned. (If reheating from cold allow 45 minutes.) Serve hot.

# LAMB AND APPLE CASSEROLE

*(Serves 4)*
450 g (1lb) potatoes
1 large onion, thinly sliced
1 large cooking apple, peeled, cored and thinly sliced
1 kg (2lb) scrag of lamb
25 g (1 oz) seedless raisins
½ level teaspoon dried mixed herbs
salt and pepper
3 level teaspoons meat extract
275 ml (½ pint) hot water
15 g (½oz) butter or margarine

1 Preheat a moderate oven (180 deg C, 350 deg F, Gas 4), centre shelf.
2 Peel and slice the potatoes thinly and soak in cold water for a few minutes to remove starch. Drain and dry on kitchen paper.
3 Cover the base of a 2.5 litre (4pint) casserole with a thin layer of potato followed by a layer of onion and some apple.
4 Put in the lamb, add the raisins, sprinkle with herbs and salt and pepper.
5 Cover with the remaining apple and onion and arrange the potatoes carefully over the top.
6 Dissolve the meat extract with the hot water and pour it into the casserole. Dot the top with small pieces of butter or margarine and cover.
7 Bake in the oven for 2 hours then uncover and cook for a further 30 minutes until the potatoes are golden.

**Oriental Crispy Fish,** see page 36

# FISH

*With nearly as much protein as meat,
and oils rich in vitamins A and D,
fish is a good basis for tasty meals
any day of the week. We used it fresh
and suggest how your fishmonger can
help you prepare it, and we also used
frozen packs for speed and convenience*

## COD CAPERS

*(Serves 4)*
**175 ml (6fl oz) milk**
**225 g (8oz) smoked cod fillet**
**1 tablespoon capers, chopped**
**25 g (1oz) butter**
**25 g (1oz) plain flour**
**salt and pepper**
**397 g (14oz) packet frozen puff pastry, thawed**

**1** Preheat a hot oven (230 deg C, 450 deg F, Gas 8), shelf in centre.
**2** Pour milk into a shallow pan with a lid, put in the smoked cod, cover and simmer for 10 minutes, until it's cooked.
**3** Then remove the fish from the pan, reserving the liquor. Skin, bone and flake the flesh.
**4** Melt the butter in a small saucepan, add the flour and cook for 3 minutes. Remove from heat. Gradually blend in the reserved fish liquor, stirring continuously. Return the sauce to the heat and simmer for 2 minutes.
**5** Add fish and capers to the sauce, season with pepper and salt if required, and allow to cool.
**6** Roll the pastry out on a lightly floured surface, and trim to an oblong approximately 25 by 38 cm (10 by 15in). Cut into 6 squares.
**7** Divide the cooled fish mixture between the 6 squares. Moisten the edges and seal together to give 6 triangles.
**8** Place on a baking sheet and cook for about 10 minutes.

## CREAMY LEMON PLAICE

*(Serves 4)*
**1 lemon**
**8 small fillets plaice**
**250 ml (½ pint) milk**
**25 g (1oz) butter or margarine**
**25 g (1oz) plain flour**
**salt and pepper**
**2 tablespoons single cream**

**1** Cut 4 thin slices from the lemon and cut each slice in half across the centre.
**2** Wrap a fillet of plaice round each piece of lemon, folding the fish with the skin inside.
**3** Place the fillets in a frying pan and pour the milk over. Bring to the boil, reduce heat and simmer gently for 5-7 minutes to cook the fish.
**4** Drain the fish, lifting each piece carefully from the pan, and arrange on a heated serving dish; keep hot. Keep the milk in the pan.
**5** Melt the butter or margarine in a small saucepan and stir in the flour. Cook gently for 3 minutes. Blend in the milk from the fish pan and bring to the boil, stirring all the time. Simmer for 2 minutes.
**6** Finely grate the rind and squeeze the juice from the remaining lemon and add to the sauce. Season well and stir in the cream.
**7** Pour sauce over the fish and serve. Remove lemon slices from inside the fish when eating.

## ORIENTAL CRISPY FISH

*(Serves 4-6)*
**40 g (1½oz) butter**
**1 large onion, sliced**
**700 g (1½lb) green cabbage, finely sliced**
**341 g (12oz) can pineapple rings**
**2 tablespoons clear honey**
**2 tablespoons wine vinegar**
**2 teaspoons soy sauce**
**1 level tablespoon cornflour**
**two 198 g (7oz) cartons crispy cod fries**
**salt and pepper**

**1** Melt the butter in a frying pan, or a large saucepan with a lid. Add onion and cabbage, cover the pan and cook slowly without burning for 15-20 minutes over a low heat, stirring occasionally.
**2** Strain pineapple juice into a measuring jug and make up to 175 ml (6fl oz) with water. Pour juice into a small saucepan with honey, vinegar and soy sauce. Heat the mixture gently.
**3** Blend the cornflour with a little water until smooth. Stir the juice mixture into the cornflour, return to the pan and bring to the boil. Simmer for 3 minutes.
**4** Meanwhile cook the cod fries according to directions on the packets. Drain well.
**5** Cut the pineapple into pieces, add to the cabbage and heat through. Season.
**6** Arrange the cabbage on hot serving dish with drained cod fries on top. Spoon a little sauce over the dish and serve the rest separately.

*See picture on page 34*

## COD DUCHESSE

*(Serves 4)*
**25 g (1oz) butter**
**25 g (1oz) plain flour**
**½ packet leek soup**
**250 ml (½ pint) milk**
**397 g (14oz) packet frozen cod steaks**
**1 egg**
**450 g (1lb) potatoes, sliced**
**a little milk and butter**
**salt and pepper**
**½ small packet potato crisps**

**1** Melt the butter in a small saucepan. Add the flour and cook gently for 3 minutes. Stir in the soup powder and

gradually blend in the milk, stirring continuously. Bring to the boil and simmer for 3 minutes.
**2** Cut each cod steak into 8 cubes, and add to the sauce. Cover and simmer for 10 minutes.
**3** Hard-boil the egg for 10 minutes, then shell and chop.
**4** Meanwhile cook the potatoes in boiling salted water until tender. Then drain and mash the potatoes with a little milk and butter.
**5** Add the egg to the fish mixture with salt and pepper and turn into a pie dish. Fork or pipe the mashed potato round the edge of the dish.
**6** Preheat a hot grill
**7** Crush the potato crisps and sprinkle in the centre of the pie. Brown under the grill, and serve at once.

## SHRIMPY PLAICE

*(Serves 2)*
**2 whole plaice, heads and fins removed (ask the**
  **fishmonger to do this)**
**25 g (1oz) butter**
**salt and pepper**
**57 g (2oz) carton potted shrimps**
**juice of ½ lemon**
**1 level tablespoon chopped parsley**

**1** Preheat a moderate grill.
**2** Place fish in grill pan with rack removed. Put a knob of butter on each, and season with salt and pepper.
**3** Grill gently until cooked through—about 10-15 minutes, according to thickness, turning once. Then remove fish and keep hot.
**4** Place the potted shrimps carefully in the grill pan, breaking them up with a fork if necessary, and heat through. Add salt and pepper, lemon juice and parsley.
**5** Pour the shrimp sauce over the fish and serve hot.

## KEDGEREE

*(Serves 4)*
**450 g (1lb) smoked cod fillet or whiting**
**3 eggs**
**225 g (8oz) long-grain rice**
**75 g (3oz) butter**
**salt and pepper**
**1 tablespoon chopped parsley**
**paprika**

**1** Place the fish in a shallow pan and cover with water. Poach for 5-8 minutes until cooked.
**2** Drain the fish; skin, bone, and flake the flesh.

**3** Meanwhile, hard-boil the eggs for 8-10 minutes. Cool under cold water, shell and roughly chop.

**4** Cook the rice in plenty of fast boiling salted water for about 12 minutes or until tender. Drain well and rinse in hot water.

**5** Melt the butter in a large saucepan and add the fish, eggs and rice. Heat through, stirring gently, and season. Stir in the parsley.

**6** Pile on to a hot serving dish and sprinkle with paprika.

## HAKE WITH CUCUMBER

*(Serves 4)*
**700 g (1½lb) hake fillet**
**seasoned flour, to coat**
**50 g (2oz) butter**
**150 ml (5fl oz) natural yogurt**
**5 cm (2in) length of cucumber, diced**
**2 tablespoons chopped chives**
**salt and pepper**

**1** Coat the hake with seasoned flour.

**2** Melt the butter in a frying pan, add the fish and fry lightly for 10-15 minutes, turning once, till cooked.

**3** Place the yogurt in a small bowl, and add the cucumber and chopped chives. Season and mix well.

**4** Remove fish from pan and drain. Place on a serving dish and pour the sauce over. Serve at once.

## HALIBUT IN THE BAG

*(Serves 4)*
**50 g (2oz) butter**
**1 large onion, sliced**
**4 tomatoes, chopped**
**1 can flat anchovy fillets**
**salt and pepper**
**4 halibut steaks**
**1 teaspoon lemon juice**
**1 tablespoon chopped parsley to garnish**

**1** Preheat a moderate oven (180 deg C, 350 deg F, Gas 4), centre shelf. Butter 4 individual pieces of kitchen foil to make 'bags' for the fish.

**2** Melt the butter in a frying pan and add the onion. Cook for about 10 minutes until soft.

**3** Drain the anchovies and cut each one in half, then add with the tomatoes to the pan. Season to taste and mix well together.

**4** Divide this mixture between the pieces of foil. Trim the fish if necessary and place on the vegetable mixture.

**5** Pour over any butter left in the frying pan, sprinkle a little lemon juice on each piece of fish and season lightly.

**6** Fold up the pieces of foil to enclose the fish completely. Place on a baking sheet or in a roasting tin and bake for 15-20 minutes till cooked—time depending on the thickness of the fish.

**7** Arrange the foil 'bags' on a heated dish. Open up and sprinkle each with parsley. Serve hot.

*See picture on page 39*

## HALIBUT WITH LEMON HERB BUTTER

*(Serves 3)*
**salt and pepper**
**3 halibut steaks**
**50 g (2oz) butter**
**1½ tablespoons fresh chopped herbs—parsley, chives, dill or thyme**
**1 tablespoon lemon juice**

**1** Preheat a moderate grill and remove rack from grill pan.

**2** Season the fish. Melt the butter in the grill pan and place the fish in it.

**3** Grill gently, turning once, for about 15 minutes, depending on thickness. Then lift fish on to a hot serving dish and keep warm.

**4** Add chosen herbs, seasoning and lemon juice to butter in the grill pan. Heat through and spoon the herby butter over the fish.

**5** Serve at once.

**Piquant Tuna Risotto,** see page 40

**Halibut in the Bag,** see page 37

## PIQUANT TUNA RISOTTO

*(Serves 4)*
**2 tablespoons cooking oil**
**1 large onion, chopped**
**225 g (8oz) long-grain rice**
**400 ml (¾ pint) chicken stock**
**150 ml (¼ pint) white wine**
**1 tablespoon finely chopped parsley**
**4 large tomatoes, peeled and chopped**
**198 g (7oz) can tuna steak**
**8 stuffed olives, chopped**
**1 level tablespoon capers**
**1 level teaspoon finely grated lemon rind**
**freshly ground black pepper**

**1** Heat the oil in a heavy pan and gently fry onion and rice for 5 minutes.
**2** Stir in stock, wine and parsley, bring to the boil. Cover and simmer gently for about 15 minutes or until the liquid is absorbed and the rice is just tender.
**3** Stir in tomatoes, drained and roughly flaked tuna, olives, capers and lemon rind and season well with pepper.
**4** Replace lid and heat through gently for 5 minutes until piping hot.

*See picture on page 38*

## ROSY FISH LOAF

*(Serves 4)*
**450 g (1lb) fresh cod fillet**
**1 small onion, grated**
**1 clove garlic, crushed**
**1 tablespoon chopped parsley**
**3 eggs, lightly beaten**
**3 tablespoons milk**
**50 g (2oz) fresh white breadcrumbs**
**salt and pepper**
**TOMATO SAUCE**
**25 g (1oz) butter**
**1 small onion, chopped**
**2 rashers streaky bacon, trimmed and chopped**
**450 g (1lb) tomatoes roughly chopped**
**½ teaspoon mixed herbs**
**salt and pepper**

**1** Preheat a moderate oven (180 deg C, 350 deg F, Gas 4), centre shelf. Grease a 450 g (1lb) loaf tin.
**2** Place cod in a frying pan, just cover with water and poach for 10-15 minutes till tender.

**3** Drain the fish. Remove skin and bones, and flake flesh into a mixing bowl. Add onion, garlic and parsley and mix well.
**4** Add the eggs, milk, breadcrumbs and seasoning to the fish mixture and blend in well.
**5** Place this mixture in the loaf tin, cover the tin with greased foil and place in a baking tin half filled with cold water.
**6** Bake in the centre of the oven for 1¼ hours, or until the mixture is set.
**7 To make the tomato sauce:** Meanwhile melt the butter in a saucepan and fry the onion and bacon until soft but not brown.
**8** Add the tomatoes and herbs to the pan, cover and simmer for 25 minutes, then sieve and return to rinsed pan. Reheat and season to taste.
**9** Turn the loaf out from the tin on to a hot serving dish. Serve the hot sauce separately.

## HARVEST FISH PIE

*(Serves 4-5)*
**500 g (1¼lb) fresh haddock fillet**
**1 medium-sized onion**
**125 g (4oz) tomatoes**
**25 g (1oz) butter**
**25 g (1oz) flour**
**150 ml (¼ pint) milk**
**190 g (7oz) can sweetcorn**
**salt and pepper**
**213 g (7½oz) packet frozen puff pastry, thawed**
**egg yolk and milk to glaze**

**1** Preheat a hot oven (220 deg C, 425 deg F, Gas 7), shelf above centre.
**2** Place fish in a frying pan, just cover with water and poach for 10 minutes.
**3** Drain the fish and reserve 150 ml (¼ pint) of liquor. Skin the fish and flake the flesh.
**4** Chop onion and cook in a little water until soft.
**5** Skin the tomatoes, cut in quarters and remove seeds.
**6** Melt the butter in a small saucepan, add flour and cook for 3 minutes. Stir in the milk and the reserved fish liquor, bring to the boil and simmer for 2 minutes, stirring continuously.
**7** Drain the sweetcorn and add half to the sauce. Then add fish, tomatoes and onion and season to taste.
**8** Turn the fish mixture into a round 23 cm (9in) pie dish and allow to cool.
**9** Roll out the pastry on a lightly floured surface, making it just bigger than the dish. Cut a circular 1 cm (½in) strip from the edge of the pastry.
**10** Damp the edge of the pie dish and fit on the pastry strip. Damp this strip and place the circle of pastry on top. Seal, trim and crimp the edges. Cut some pastry leaves from the trimmings.

11 Make a hole in the centre of pie. Brush with beaten egg and milk to glaze, arrange the leaves on top and brush with more glaze.

12 Bake in the oven for 15-20 minutes until golden.

13 Serve at once, using the remaining sweetcorn mixed with peas as a vegetable.

## PARSLEY FISH CAKES

*(Serves 4)*

350 g (12oz) smoked haddock fillet, skinned (ask the fishmonger to do this)
2 large hard-boiled eggs
1 (2-3 serving) packet instant mashed potato
2 level teaspoons chopped parsley
salt and pepper
a little plain flour
1 egg, beaten
2 small packets potato crisps, lightly crushed
50 g (2oz) cooking fat

1 Cut the fish into even-sized pieces and place in a frying pan. Just cover with water and poach fillets gently for about 12 minutes, until cooked.

2 Drain the fish and flake the flesh into a bowl. Coarsely chop the eggs and add to the fish.

3 Make up the potato as directed on the packet and stir into the fish mixture. Add the chopped parsley, plenty of pepper, and salt if needed.

4 Using a little flour, shape the mixture into 8 cakes.

5 Pour the beaten egg on to one plate, the crushed potato crisps on to another and dip each fish cake first into egg then into crisps to coat.

6 Heat the cooking fat in a large frying pan and fry the fish-cakes for 5 minutes on each side, until golden brown, turning the fish cakes over carefully with a fish slice.

7 Drain well on kitchen paper and serve hot with a crisp green salad.

## TIPSY HADDOCK

*(Serves 4)*

700 g (1½lb) fresh haddock fillet, skinned
salt and pepper
1 small onion, finely sliced
100 g (40oz) button mushrooms, sliced
150 ml (¼ pint) cider
15 g (½oz) butter
15 g (½oz) plain flour
1 small packet potato crisps
50 g (2oz) grated cheese

1 Preheat a moderately hot oven (190 deg C, 375 deg F, Gas 5), shelf towards top.

2 Cut the haddock into 2.5 cm (1in) wide strips, place in a 1.15 litre (2 pint) shallow ovenproof dish and season well with salt and pepper.

3 Add onion, mushrooms and cider to fish and cover with foil or a lid.

4 Cook in the oven for 40 minutes.

5 Meanwhile cream together the butter and flour ready for thickening the sauce.

6 Take the dish from the oven and pour liquid off into a small pan. Keep the fish on one side, covered, and raise the oven temperature to hot (230 deg C, 450 deg F, Gas 8), top shelf.

7 Bring the reserved liquid to the boil and, using a wooden spoon, gradually blend in small spoonfuls of the thickening mixture until the sauce is thick enough to coat the back of the spoon. Then boil quickly for 2-3 minutes, stirring continuously, to cook the flour. Then pour over the fish.

8 Sprinkle with broken potato crisps, then with the grated cheese. Return to the oven for 5-8 minutes to melt and brown the cheese.

9 Serve hot, from the dish.

## TROUT ANGLAISE

*(Serves 2)*

2 frozen rainbow trout, thawed
2 medium-sized tomatoes
25 g (1oz) butter
1 small onion, finely chopped
5 cm (2in) piece of cucumber, peeled and diced
sprigs of fresh tarragon
    or 1 tablespoon finely chopped parsley
4 tablespoons apple juice

1 Preheat a moderately hot oven (190 deg C, 375 deg F, Gas 5), centre shelf.

2 Wash the trout, trim the fins and tails with a pair of scissors, remove the eyes, if preferred. Lightly butter an ovenproof dish and place the trout in it.

3 To skin the tomatoes: place in a bowl and cover with boiling water for a few seconds, drain and cover with cold water, then strip off skins. Cut the tomatoes into quarters and remove the seeds. Then chop the tomato flesh into coarse dice.

4 Melt the butter in a small pan. Add the onion and cook slowly without browning—about 5 minutes. Then add the tomato and cucumber and cook together gently for a further 2 minutes.

5 Place washed sprigs of tarragon (if using) in the oven-proof dish and arrange the trout on top. Add the apple juice and parsley (if using) to the vegetable mixture and pour over the trout.

6 Cover the dish with foil and bake in the oven for 30 minutes until fish is cooked.

7 Serve hot from the dish.

# COD FRITTERS WITH LEMON MAYONNAISE

*(Serves 4)*
**500 g (1¼lb) thick end of cod fillet,
  skinned and boned (ask the fishmonger to do this)
seasoned flour, to coat
1 egg, beaten
dried white breadcrumbs, to coat
fat or oil for deep frying
LEMON MAYONNAISE
grated rind 1 lemon
1 tablespoon lemon juice
150 ml (¼ pint) real mayonnaise
salt and pepper
1 tablespoon chopped parsley**

**1** Cut the fish into bite-sized pieces.
**2** Place the flour, egg and breadcrumbs on separate dishes. Dip the fish in the flour, shaking off excess, then dip in egg and coat in breadcrumbs. Place in fridge to allow coating to set.
**3 To make lemon mayonnaise:** Meanwhile blend lemon rind and juice with the mayonnaise, salt and pepper, and chopped parsley.
**4** Heat the oil in a deep frying pan. Fry fish fairly quickly until golden and cooked, about 3-5 minutes. Drain well on kitchen paper.
**5** Serve at once with mayonnaise and chips or a salad.

*See picture right*

**Cod Fritters with Lemon Mayonnaise,** see opposite

# FISH MADRAS

*(Serves 4)*
**25 g (1oz) butter or margarine**
**1 medium-sized onion, finely chopped**
**1 level tablespoon curry powder**
**1 teaspoon curry paste**
**1½ tablespoons plain flour**
**400 ml (¾ pint) chicken stock, or water and a stock cube**
**1 level tablespoon dessicated coconut**
**1 level tablespoon redcurrant jelly**
**1 level tablespoon mango chutney**
**5 peppercorns**
**8 fillets of plaice, skinned (ask the fishmonger to do this, or follow Step 3 below).**
**25 g (1oz) parsley and thyme stuffing mix**
**salt and pepper**
**juice of ½ lemon**
**1 egg**
**golden breadcrumbs**
**fat or oil for deep frying**

**1** To make the sauce, melt the butter and gently fry the onion for about 5 minutes. Add the curry powder and cook for 3 minutes. Then stir in the curry paste and flour and cook gently for a further 2 minutes.
**2** Mix the stock, coconut, redcurrant jelly, chutney and peppercorns together and gradually blend into the mixture in the pan. Cover and simmer for 30 minutes, then strain the sauce into a bowl and return to a clean pan.
**3** If the fish needs to be skinned, do it as follows: holding the tail of a fillet, cut through the flesh at the tail end, and with a sawing action, cut and push the flesh off the skin. Repeat for all fillets.
**4** Make up the stuffing using 4 tablespoons boiling water.
**5** Place the fillets, skinned side uppermost, on a chopping board, season and sprinkle with a little lemon juice. Divide the stuffing between the fillets, placing it at the widest end. Fold the fillets in half, folding a little of the tail piece first, and flatten them to a neat shape.
**6** Break the egg on to a plate; add 1½ tablespoons cold water. Place the prepared breadcrumbs on another plate.
**7** Dip the fillets into the egg mixture and then into the crumbs. Press the crumbs on carefully and repeat for other fillets. Coat each fillet twice.
**8** Heat the fat or oil. Fry the fillets gently for 10 minutes, drain and arrange on a serving dish.
**9** Meanwhile reheat the sauce and pour over fish.
**10** Serve with plain boiled rice, and serve sliced bananas, redcurrant jelly and desiccated coconut separately.

## SMOKED FISH FLAN

*(Serves 4)*
213 g (7½oz) packet frozen shortcrust pastry, thawed
213 g (7½oz) packet frozen smoked haddock
  fillets, thawed
250 ml (½ pint) milk
1 bay leaf
4 peppercorns
1 small carrot, peeled
25 g (1oz) butter
25 g (1oz) plain flour
salt and pepper
1 small onion, finely chopped
1 hard-boiled egg, sliced
40 g (1½oz) Cheddar cheese, grated

1 Preheat a moderately hot oven (220 deg C, 400 deg F, Gas 6), shelf above centre. Place a 20 cm (8in) flan ring on a baking sheet.
2 Roll out the pastry on a floured surface, and use to line the flan ring, pressing well into the base. Prick the base with a fork. Line the flan with greaseproof paper and fill with baking beans or rice.
3 Bake blind in the oven for 15 minutes. Then remove the greaseproof paper and beans or rice and return the flan to the oven and cook for a further 10 minutes. Then remove and place on an ovenproof plate.
4 Meanwhile poach the fish in a little water, according to the directions on the packet. Then drain, remove the skin and bone and flake the flesh.
5 Put the milk in a saucepan with the bay leaf, peppercorns and carrot and place over a low heat for about 20 minutes to extract the flavours. Do not boil. Then strain the milk into a measuring jug, discarding carrot, bay leaf, and peppercorns.
6 Rinse out the saucepan and add the butter and allow to melt. Stir in the flour and cook without browning for 3 minutes. Gradually blend in the infused milk, stirring continuously. Simmer for 2 minutes, and season to taste.
7 Arrange the flaked fish and chopped onion in the flan. Place the egg on top, and coat with the sauce.
8 Preheat a moderate grill. Sprinkle the cheese over the flan. Grill for 5 minutes until the flan has heated through and the cheese is lightly browned.
9 Serve hot with a salad.

## KIPPER SCALLOPS

*(Serves 4)*
2 medium-sized kippers
50 g (2oz) butter
25 g (1oz) plain flour
150 ml (½ pint) milk
salt and pepper
1 teaspoon lemon juice
2 hard-boiled eggs
1 (2 serving) packet instant potato

1 Place kippers in a frying pan, just cover with water and poach for about 10 minutes.
2 Melt half the butter in a small saucepan, stir in the flour and cook for 3 minutes. Blend in the milk, bring to the boil and simmer for 2 minutes.
3 Remove skin and bone from the fish and flake the flesh. Add the fish to the sauce, season to taste and add the lemon juice.
4 Cut the hard-boiled eggs in half lengthways and place half in each of 4 scallop shells or individual dishes.
5 Pour the fish sauce over each half hard-boiled egg.
6 Make up the potato as directed on the packet, add remaining butter, season and beat well.
7 Preheat a moderate grill.
8 Place potato in a piping bag and pipe round the fish.
9 Gently grill to brown the potatoes and serve hot.

## TANGY BAKED HERRINGS

*(Serves 4)*
4 herrings, gutted and heads removed (ask the
  fishmonger to do this, or follow Step 2 below)
397 g (14oz) can peeled tomatoes
**STUFFING**
grated rind and juice of ½ lemon
50 g (2oz) fresh white breadcrumbs
1 rounded tablespoon chopped parsley
¼ level teaspoon dried mixed herbs
1 egg, lightly beaten
salt and pepper

1 Preheat a moderately hot oven (190 deg C, 375 deg F, Gas 5), centre shelf.
2 Cut the heads off the herrings, using a sharp knife. Cut along the underside of the fish and remove the intestines. Wash the fish and dry on kitchen paper.
3 **To prepare the stuffing:** Place lemon rind and juice in a small bowl, add the breadcrumbs, parsley and herbs. Stir the egg into the stuffing and season to taste. Mix well.

**4** Fill the body of the herrings with stuffing.

**5** Pour the contents of the can of tomatoes into a shallow ovenproof dish and season. Arrange the stuffed herrings on top.

**6** Bake in the oven for 25-30 minutes until fish is cooked.

**7** Serve hot from the dish.

# PRAWN CREOLE

*(Serves 3)*
125 g (4oz) long-grain rice
1 tablespoon oil
1 medium-sized onion, chopped
1 clove garlic, crushed
227 g (8oz) can peeled tomatoes
½ small green pepper, de-seeded and chopped
salt and pepper
350 g (12oz) peeled prawns
parsley to garnish

**1** Cook the rice in boiling salted water for 12 minutes, or until tender. Drain, rinse and keep hot.

**2** Heat the oil in a saucepan and add onion and garlic. Cook gently until soft but not browned—about 5 minutes.

**3** Add the tomatoes and their juice, the chopped pepper and seasoning, and simmer for 10 minutes.

**4** Add the prawns and cook gently for a further 5 minutes.

**5** Arrange the rice round the edge of a hot serving dish. Pour the sauce into the centre and garnish with parsley. Serve at once.

# SMOKED BUCKLING PÂTÉ

*(Serves 4-6)*
275-350 g (10-12oz) smoked buckling
2.5 cm (1in) thick slice white bread
150 ml (¼ pint) milk
2 level teaspoons creamed horseradish
salt
freshly ground black pepper
about 70 ml (3fl oz) soured cream
1 level tablespoon chopped parsley

**1** Skin and bone the fish, flake the flesh into a small mixing bowl.

**2** Cut the crusts off and dice the bread. Place in another small bowl and pour the milk over.

**3** Mash the fish very well with a fork, removing any large bones that become visible. Add the creamed horseradish and seasoning to taste.

**4** Remove the bread from the milk and squeeze out the excess liquid. Add to the fish with 1 tablespoon of the milk, the soured cream and the parsley.

**5** Mix all the ingredients until thoroughly blended.

**6** Pack into a suitable serving bowl or pot, and serve the pâté cold with hot buttered toast.

# MACKEREL WITH GOOSEBERRY SAUCE

*(Serves 4)*
4 small mackerel, filleted (ask the fishmonger to do this or follow Step 1 below)
2 tablespoons plain flour
salt and pepper
1 tablespoon paprika
40 g (1½oz) butter or margarine
**GOOSEBERRY SAUCE**
450 g (1lb) gooseberries, washed
1 tablespoon water
15 g (½oz) butter or margarine
4 level teaspoons sugar
salt and pepper

**1** Remove the head and tails from the fish and clean out the insides, splitting along the belly. Open out and place on a board, skin uppermost. Press down firmly along the backbone to loosen it. Turn the fish over and lift out backbone and any small bones. Cut the fillets in half lengthwise and wash. Dry on kitchen paper.

**2** Place the flour on a plate. Add seasoning and paprika to it and mix well.

**3** Press fish fillets into the flour mixture to coat. Shake off the excess.

**4** Heat the butter in a large frying pan. Fry the fish fillets gently for about 10 minutes, turning once carefully during cooking.

**5** **To make the sauce:** Meanwhile place the gooseberries in a saucepan with the water and butter and simmer gently until cooked. Then sieve or liquidise to make a purée and return to the pan. Stir in the sugar and seasoning. Reheat.

**6** Drain the fish and serve hot with the sauce.

**Perfect Prawny,** see opposite

# EGGS & CHEESE

*Versatile and nourishing, eggs and cheese are every cook's standby. They're an inexpensive source of nourishment: one egg has a similar protein value to an ounce of beef, with slightly more fat. And all the cheeses provide protein and a delicious variety of flavour*

## PERFECT PRAWNY

*(Serves 2)*
**3 tomatoes**
**40 g (1½oz) butter**
**50 g (2oz) peeled prawns**
**4 eggs**
**2 tablespoons water**
**salt and pepper**
**1 teaspoon chopped parsley**

**1** To skin the tomatoes: Place in a bowl and cover with boiling water. Leave for ½ minute, drain and cover with cold water, then strip off skins. Cut the tomatoes in half and remove seeds and liquid. Cut the flesh into wedges.
**2** Melt 25 g (1oz) of the butter in a small saucepan. Add the prawns and tomatoes and heat gently, stirring.
**3** Break the eggs into a mixing bowl and beat lightly. Add the water and seasonings.
**4** Melt the remaining butter in an omelette or frying pan, tipping the pan so that the butter coats its surface. When hot pour in the beaten eggs and cook quickly, drawing the cooked edges towards centre of the pan in the usual manner. When nearly set, spoon filling over omelette.
**5** Sprinkle with parsley and slide on to a heated serving dish. Serve at once.

*See picture opposite*

## CHEESY POTATO PIE

*(Serves 4)*
**700 g (1½lb) potatoes**
**1 medium-sized onion, thinly sliced**
**pepper**
**175 g (6oz) cheese, grated**
**about 250 ml (½ pint) milk**
**25 g (1oz) butter or margarine**

**1** Preheat a moderately hot oven (190 deg C, 375 deg F, Gas 5), centre shelf. Butter a 1¼ litre (2 pint) ovenproof dish or casserole.
**2** Peel the potatoes and cut into very thin slices.
**3** Place potato and onion slices in a saucepan of salted water and bring to the boil. Cover and simmer for 5-7 minutes until the potatoes are just soft. Drain well.
**4** Arrange half the potato and onion in the prepared dish, season well with pepper and cover with half the cheese. Then cover with remaining potato and onion, season again with pepper and sprinkle over the remaining cheese.
**5** Warm the milk and then pour it into the dish. Dot with butter or margarine and bake in the oven for 20 minutes.
**6** Then increase the oven temperature to hot (230 deg C, 450 deg F, Gas 8), and move the pie to the top shelf. Cook for a further 10 minutes until the surface is golden brown.
**7** Serve the pie piping hot with some crispy bacon rashers.

## EGG AND ASPARAGUS PUFF

*(Serves 4)*
**340 g (12oz) can asparagus spears**
**a little milk**
**15 g (½oz) butter or margarine**
**15 g (½oz) plain flour**
**8 hard-boiled eggs**
**salt and pepper**
**397 g (14oz) packet frozen puff pastry, thawed**

**1** Preheat a hot oven (230 deg C, 450 deg F, Gas 8), shelf above centre.
**2** Drain the liquor from the asparagus and if necessary make up to 150 ml (¼ pint) with milk.
**3** Melt the butter or margarine in a small saucepan, stir in the flour and cook for 3 minutes. Then blend in the asparagus liquor and bring to the boil, stirring continuously. Simmer for 2 minutes.
**4** Roughly chop the eggs and asparagus and add to the sauce. Season to taste.
**5** Roll out the pastry on a lightly floured surface to make a 30 cm (12in) square. Trim neatly, and dampen the edges with water.
**6** Place the filling in the middle, bring the 4 corners to the centre to form an envelope and seal firmly. Brush with milk and place on baking sheet.
**7** Bake in the oven for 20 minutes until the pastry is well risen and golden brown. Serve hot or cold.

## MUSHROOM SOUFFLÉ

*(Serves 4-6)*
**75 g (3oz) butter**
**175 g (6oz) mushrooms, chopped**
**50 g (2oz) plain flour**
**250 ml (½ pint) milk**
**salt and freshly ground black pepper**
**mushroom ketchup**
**4 large eggs**

**1** Preheat a moderately hot oven (190 deg C, 375 deg F, Gas 5), centre shelf. Lightly butter and flour a 1¼ litre (2-2½ pint) soufflé dish, and place on a baking sheet.
**2** Melt 25 g (1oz) of the butter in a medium-sized saucepan and fry the mushrooms until soft—about 3 minutes. Lift out with a draining spoon and drain mushrooms on kitchen paper.
**3** Melt the remaining butter in the saucepan, add the flour, and cook slowly without browning for 2 minutes. Gradually blend in the milk, and slowly bring to the boil, stirring continuously.

**4** Remove from the heat, stir in the mushrooms, season to taste, and add a few drops of mushroom ketchup. Allow the mixture to cool for 5 minutes.
**5** Separate the eggs and beat the yolks into the sauce.
**6** Place the whites in a large bowl, and whisk until stiff and standing in peaks. Then carefully fold the whites into the sauce mixture with a large metal spoon until evenly distributed.
**7** Pour the mixture into the prepared dish. Bake in the oven for 35 minutes. (Do not open the oven door while the soufflé is cooking.)
**8** Remove the soufflé from the oven and serve at once.

## SWEETCORN EGG BAKE

*(Serves 1)*
**198 g (7oz) can sweetcorn**
**1 slice ham, chopped**
**1 large egg**
**1 tablespoon top milk**
**a small knob of butter**
**salt and pepper**

**1** Preheat a moderate oven (180 deg C, 350 deg F, Gas 4), centre shelf.
**2** Drain the sweetcorn and place in a small ovenproof dish. Mix in the ham and make a slight hollow in the centre of the mixture.
**3** Break the egg into the hollow in the sweetcorn mixture. Spoon the milk over, dot the butter on the egg yolk and season with salt and pepper.
**4** Bake in the oven for about 15-20 minutes until the egg is just set. Serve hot.
**Note.** This is a good dish to make when you are using the oven for other cooking.

## EGG AND BACON JACKS

*(Makes 8)*
**4 round crusty bread rolls, warmed**
**butter for spreading**
**TOPPING**
**knob of butter**
**1 very small onion, thinly sliced**
**4-6 rashers of streaky bacon, trimmed and finely diced**
**50 g (2oz) button mushrooms, sliced**
**SCRAMBLED EGGS**
**4 large eggs**
**3 tablespoons milk**
**salt and pepper**
**knob of butter**

1 **To prepare the topping:** Melt the butter in a small pan and fry the onion for 5 minutes until just turning brown. Add the bacon and fry for 2 minutes.

2 Stir in the mushrooms, adding a little more butter if necessary and fry gently, stirring frequently, for 5-7 minutes until mushrooms are cooked. Keep warm.

3 Meanwhile, break the eggs into a mixing bowl and whisk in the milk and seasoning.

4 **To scramble eggs:** Melt the butter in a pan and pour in the eggs. Heat gently, stirring all the time, until the eggs are lightly scrambled.

5 Cut the warm rolls in half and spread with butter. Divide the scrambled egg between them. Place a spoonful of topping in the centre of each one. Serve at once.

## PIPERADE

*(Serves 3-4)*
**2 medium-sized green peppers**
**1 large onion, sliced**
**2 tablespoons oil**
**225 g (8oz) tomatoes**
**2 canned red peppers, sliced**
**6-8 eggs**
**salt and pepper**

1 Remove stalks, seeds and white pith from the peppers. Cut the flesh into thin strips.

2 Heat the oil in a large frying pan and add the onion and peppers. Cook gently, stirring occasionally, until soft but not brown—about 15 minutes

3 To skin the tomatoes: Meanwhile place in a bowl and cover with boiling water. Leave for ½ minute, drain and cover with cold water; strip off skins. Then remove all seeds and liquid and cut tomato flesh into strips.

4 Add the tomatoes and red peppers to the frying pan and cook gently for about 3 minutes, stirring occasionally.

5 Beat the eggs in a bowl with seasoning to taste.

6 Pour into the pan and cook over medium heat stirring continuously until the eggs are lightly scrambled. Transfer on to a heated serving dish and serve immediately.

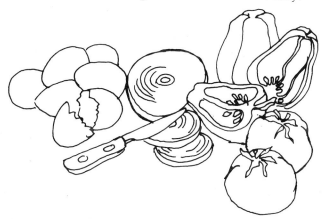

## EGG SUPPER DISH

*(Serves 3-4)*
**6 large eggs**
**298 g (10½oz) can condensed asparagus soup**
**4 tablespoons top milk**
**3 thin slices white bread**
**50 g (2oz) cheese, grated**
**parsley to garnish**

1 Place the eggs in a small saucepan of boiling water and boil for 7 minutes until set but not hard.

2 Meanwhile empty the can of soup into a saucepan and stir in the top milk. Heat gently, stirring, until almost at boiling point.

3 Preheat a hot grill and toast the bread lightly on both sides. Cut into 12 triangles and keep warm.

4 Shell the eggs and cut in half lengthways. Place them cut side down in a shallow ovenproof dish. Coat evenly with the soup and sprinkle the cheese over.

5 Grill until the top is brown and bubbling.

6 Arrange the toast triangles round the edge of the dish and garnish with parsley.

## SUNNYSIDE JACKETS

*(Serves 2-4)*
**2 large potatoes**
**butter for greasing**
**salt and pepper**
**15 g (½oz) butter**
**4 eggs**

1 Preheat a hot oven (220 deg C, 425 deg F, Gas 7), shelf above centre.

2 Wash the potatoes thoroughly and rub all over with butter. Place on a baking sheet and bake for 1 hour, or until soft.

3 Remove potatoes from the oven and reduce the temperature to moderate (180 deg C, 350 deg F, Gas 4).

4 Cut the potatoes in half lengthways and carefully scoop the flesh out into a basin. Keep the jackets.

5 Add salt, pepper and butter to the potato and mash well with a fork until soft. Spoon this mixture back into the jackets, making a hollow in the centre of each half with the back of a spoon. Replace the filled jackets on the baking tray.

6 Break the eggs one at a time into a cup and carefully tip one into each potato half.

7 Return to the oven for about 10 minutes—until the eggs are just set. Serve immediately.

# EGG AND BACON CROQUETTES

*(Serves 4)*
**7 eggs**
**225 g (8oz) streaky bacon, trimmed and chopped**
**75 g (3oz) butter or margarine**
**75 g (3oz) plain flour**
**400 ml (¾ pint) milk**
**salt and pepper**
**oil or fat for deep frying**
**sprig of parsley or lemon wedges to garnish**
**COATING**
**1 egg**
**1 tablespoon milk**
**about 50 g (2oz) dried breadcrumbs**
**1 tablespoon plain flour**

**1** Hard-boil 6 eggs, 8-10 minutes. Drain, cover with cold water and leave to cool.
**2** Gently fry the bacon in a small saucepan until cooked. Drain off bacon fat, add the butter and melt. Stir in the flour and cook gently for 3 minutes. Then blend in the milk and bring to the boil, stirring continuously. Simmer for 2 minutes, then remove from heat, season, and stir in the remaining egg.
**3** Shell and chop the hard-boiled eggs and stir into the sauce. Turn the mixture on to a plate to cool.
**4** When cold, divide the mixture into 8 portions and shape into long croquettes.
**5 To coat:** Break the egg on to a plate and beat lightly with the milk. Put crumbs and flour on separate plates. Coat each croquette lightly in flour, dip in egg, drain, and roll in the crumbs.
**6** Heat deep pan of oil or fat till a bread cube dropped in browns in ½ minute. Keep over medium heat.
**7** Place half the croquettes in the frying basket, and lower carefully into the oil. Cook each batch for 4-5 minutes; drain well.
**8** Serve hot, garnished with parsley or lemon.

*See picture opposite*

**Egg and Bacon Croquettes,** see opposite

51

## EGGS KATRINA

*(Serves 4)*
**225 g (8oz) long-grain rice**
**6 eggs**
**40 g (1½oz) butter or margarine**
**40 g (1½oz) plain flour**
**400 ml (¾ pint) milk**
**1 green pepper**
**125 g (4oz) peeled prawns**
**salt and pepper**

1 Cook the rice in plenty of boiling salted water until tender—about 12 minutes. Drain and rinse under hot water. Keep hot.
2 Hard-boil the eggs for 12 minutes, shell and cut in half lengthways.
3 Meanwhile, melt the butter or margarine in a small saucepan and stir in the flour. Cook gently for 3 minutes. Gradually blend in the milk and bring to the boil, stirring continuously. Simmer for 2 minutes.
4 De-seed the green pepper and cut the flesh into thin strips. Place in a bowl and cover with boiling water. Leave to stand for 2 minutes then drain well.
5 Stir the pepper strips and the prawns into the sauce, season to taste and heat through.
6 Place the rice in a border round the edge of a heated serving plate and arrange the eggs in the centre. Pour the sauce over and serve at once.

## FLUFFY HERBED MUSHROOM OMELETTE

*(Serves 1)*
**2 eggs**
**onion or celery salt, and pepper**
**25 g (1oz) butter**
**50 g (2oz) mushrooms, sliced**
**a good pinch of dried mixed herbs**
**1 teaspoon chopped parsley**

1 Separate the egg yolks from the whites and place in different bowls. Stir seasoning into the egg yolks.
2 Melt most of the butter in a small saucepan. Add the mushrooms and cook gently, stirring occasionally. Keep hot over a low heat.
3 Preheat a hot grill.
5 Whisk the egg whites until stiff and standing in peaks. Fold in the yolks using a metal spoon.
5 Heat the remaining knob of butter in a small omelette pan, tipping the pan so that the butter coats its surface.

Pour in the fluffy egg mixture and spread out evenly in the pan. Cook slowly until the underside is just brown and the sides are beginning to set.
6 Sprinkle the surface of the omelette with the herbs and grill until the top is golden brown.
7 Quickly cut a slit across the centre with a knife. Spoon on the mushrooms and chopped parsley and fold over.
8 Slide on to a hot plate and serve at once.

## SAVOURY EGG FLAN

*(Serves 4-6)*
**SHORTCRUST PASTRY**
**175 g (6oz) plain flour**
**½ level teaspoon salt**
**75 g (3oz) butter or margarine**
**cold water to mix**
**FILLING**
**3 large eggs**
**salt and pepper**
**125 g (4oz) lean streaky bacon, trimmed and diced**
**50 g (2oz) button mushrooms, sliced**

1 Preheat a moderate oven (180 deg C, 350 deg F, Gas 4), shelf above centre. Place a 20 cm (8in) flan ring on a baking sheet, or use a sandwich tin.
2 **To make the pastry:** Sift the flour and salt into a mixing bowl. Add the butter or margarine and rub in, using the fingertips, until the mixture resembles fine breadcrumbs. Mix to a firm dough with a little water.
3 Roll out on a lightly floured surface. Line the flan ring or tin with the pastry and trim the edges. Prick the base, and line with greaseproof paper, fill with baking beans.
4 Bake in the oven for 10 minutes until the pastry is set.
5 **To make the filling:** Meanwhile, whisk the eggs in a bowl and add seasoning, bacon and mushrooms.
6 Pour carefully into pastry flan case and return to centre of the oven for 30-40 minutes, until filling has set.
7 Serve hot or cold.

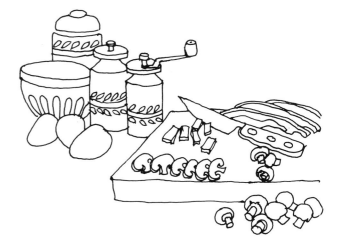

## CHEESE AND POTATO PATS

*(Serves 4)*
**1 (4-serving) packet instant potato**
**50 g (2oz) cooked ham or bacon, finely chopped**
**175 g (6oz) cheese, grated**
**1 level tablespoon chopped chives or parsley**
**salt and pepper**
**a little flour**
**1 egg**
**dried breadcrumbs for coating**
**fat or oil for frying**
**2 sliced tomatoes to garnish**

1 Make up the mashed potato as directed on the packet and allow to cool.
2 When cold mix in ham or bacon, cheese, chives or parsley, and season to taste.
3 Using a little flour, shape the mixture into 8 round flat cakes.
4 Break the egg on to a plate and beat with a fork to mix. Spread the crumbs on a sheet of paper.
5 Dip the cakes first into the egg, drain slightly, and then coat in the crumbs.
6 Heat about 1 cm (½in) depth of cooking fat or oil in a large frying pan. Fry the cakes gently in the pan until golden brown—about 5 minutes each side. Drain well.
7 Arrange on a hot serving dish and garnish with the sliced tomatoes.

## MACARONI EGGS

*(Serves 4)*
**65 g (2½oz) butter or margarine**
**1 large Spanish onion, chopped**
**175 g (6oz) quick-cooking macaroni**
**3 tomatoes, skinned and chopped**
**40 g (1½oz) plain flour**
**425 ml (¾ pint) milk**
**1 bay leaf**
**salt and pepper**
**6-8 hard-boiled eggs, shelled**
**50 g (2oz) cheese, grated**

1 Heat 25 g (1oz) of the butter or margarine in a saucepan, add the onion and cook until soft—about 10 minutes.
2 Cook macaroni in boiling salted water until just tender—about 7 minutes. Drain well then mix into onion. Add the tomatoes, cover and keep hot.
3 Melt the remaining fat in saucepan, stir in the flour and cook for 1 minute. Blend in the milk, add bay leaf and

bring to the boil, stirring until thick. Season to taste. Remove bay leaf.
4 Preheat a moderate grill.
5 Turn the macaroni mixture into a heated heatproof dish. Halve the eggs and arrange in macaroni, cut side up. Coat with sauce and sprinkle cheese on top.
6 Grill until golden brown.

## PÂTÉ STUFFED EGGS

*(Serves 4 as a starter)*
**6 large hard-boiled eggs**
**25 g (1oz) butter, slightly softened**
**75 g (3oz) liver pâté**
**salt and pepper**
**paprika**
**GARNISH**
**1 bunch watercress, trimmed**
**4 large firm tomatoes, sliced**
**1 tablespoon vinegar**
**chopped chives**

1 Remove shells and cut eggs in half lengthways. Spoon the yolks into a small bowl. Add the slightly softened butter, liver pâté and salt and pepper. Cream ingredients together to make a smooth paste.
2 Pipe or spoon the mixture back into the halved whites and sprinkle with paprika. Arrange the eggs on a flat serving dish.
3 Garnish eggs with watercress and sliced tomato and sprinkle with vinegar and chopped chives.

## BAKED RATATOUILLE WITH EGGS

*(Serves 4 as a starter)*
**397 g (14oz) packet frozen ratatouille, thawed**
**salt and pepper**
**4 eggs**
**15 g (½oz) butter**

1 Preheat a moderate oven (180 deg C, 350 deg F, Gas 4), centre shelf. Butter a large shallow ovenproof dish.
2 Place the ratatouille in the dish and season to taste.
3 Make 4 wells in the ratatouille and break an egg into each one. Dot each egg with a small piece of butter and cover the dish with foil.
4 Bake in the oven for about 30 minutes, depending on how soft you want the eggs.
5 Serve hot from the dish.

**Prawn and Pepper Vol-au-Vents,** see opposite

54

# SNACKS

*Here are recipes to help you provide for the unexpected in as little as 15 minutes. They make tasty snacks on their own, or light meals when teamed with the salads that follow, or you can serve them as 'starters' before a main meal*

## PRAWN AND PEPPER VOL-AU-VENTS

*(Serves 6)*
75 g (3oz) butter or margarine
1 medium-sized onion, finely chopped
6 large individual vol-au-vent cases
75 g (3oz) plain flour
825 ml (1½ pints) milk
½ teaspoon tabasco sauce
salt and pepper
1 level teaspoon paprika
225-350 g (8-12oz) peeled prawns
190 g (7oz) can red peppers, drained and sliced
parsley to garnish

1 Preheat a moderately hot oven (190 deg C, 375 deg F, Gas 5), centre shelf.
2 Melt the butter or margarine in a large saucepan and add the onion. Cook gently until soft but not brown.
3 Meanwhile arrange the vol-au-vent cases on a baking sheet. Cut out the lids and leave on the baking sheet separately. Place in the oven and heat through for about ten minutes, until hot.
4 Meanwhile, add the flour to the pan and cook for 3 minutes, stirring continuously. Gradually blend in the milk and bring to the boil, stirring all the time. Simmer gently for 2 minutes. Add tabasco, seasoning, paprika, prawns and red peppers. Heat mixture gently, stirring continuously.
5 Place vol-au-vent cases on individual plates, fill with the hot sauce, and replace the lids.
6 Garnish with parsley and serve at once.

*See picture opposite*

## GOLDEN ROE BOATS

*(Serves 4)*
4 large slices brown bread
450 g (1lb) freshly boiled cod's roe
plain flour, seasoned
75 g (3oz) butter
2 tablespoons lemon juice

1 Preheat a hot grill.
2 Toast the bread on one side only.
3 Remove the skin from the roe and cut into 1 cm (½in) thick slices. Coat with seasoned flour.
4 Melt 50 g (2oz) butter in a large frying pan and fry the roe slices for about 10 minutes, turning once.
5 Place the slices of toast on 4 plates; put the portions of roe on untoasted sides.
6 Add the 25 g (1oz) butter to the pan and heat until just beginning to brown. Add the lemon juice, reheat and pour a little over each portion. Serve hot.

## DEEP SOUTH BACON FRY

(Serves 4)
**175 g (6oz) frozen sweetcorn**
**3 large eggs**
**2 tablespoons milk**
**salt and pepper**
**about 75 g (3oz) dripping or cooking fat**
**4 fairly thick slices of bread**
**8 rashers streaky bacon, trimmed**
**15 g (½oz) butter**

1 Cook sweetcorn according to packet directions. Drain in a colander.
2 Whisk the eggs, milk and seasoning together in a bowl and stir in the sweetcorn.
3 Heat half the dripping or cooking fat in a large frying pan until hot and fry the bread quickly on both sides until brown and crisp.
4 Add more dripping and fry remaining slices. Drain well on kitchen paper and keep hot.
5 Fry bacon on both sides. Keep hot with the fried bread.
6 Clean the pan. Add the butter and allow to melt.
7 Pour in the sweetcorn mixture and stir gently with a wooden spoon until lightly scrambled. Stop stirring and brown lightly on underside. Cut into 4 wedges.
8 To serve, place a slice of bread on each plate. Cover them with bacon, lift a portion of sweetcorn, browned side uppermost, on to each slice and serve at once while still piping hot.

## JACKET POTATO POP-UPS

(Serves 4)
**4 medium-sized potatoes**
**about 50 g (1oz) butter**
**salt and pepper**
**1 medium-sized onion, thinly sliced**
**225 g (8oz) streaky or back bacon, trimmed and chopped**
**50 g (2oz) cheese, grated**
**watercress to garnish**

1 Preheat a hot oven (220 deg C, 425 deg F, Gas 7), shelf above centre.
2 Scrub the potatoes thoroughly and wipe dry. Rub all over with a little butter and sprinkle with salt.
3 Place on a baking sheet; bake for about 1 hour—until soft. Remove from the oven and raise the temperature to very hot (230 deg C, 450 deg F, Gas 8), shelf towards top.
4 Meanwhile, melt the remaining butter in a pan and gently fry the onion until soft and brown.

5 Add the bacon to the onion and fry gently for 2-3 minutes to extract the fat.
6 Cut the potatoes in half lengthways and scoop the potato into the pan with the onion and bacon, keeping the jackets whole. Mix well.
7 Season the potato mixture and pile back into the jackets. Top each half with a little grated cheese. Place on a baking sheet and return to the oven for 6-8 minutes to melt the cheese and lightly brown the top.
8 Garnish with watercress and serve.

## TOAST AND CHEESE PUDDING

(Serves 4)
**4 slices bread from a medium-sliced sandwich loaf**
**butter for spreading**
**a little French mustard**
**225 g (8oz) Cheddar cheese, grated**
**250 ml (½ pint) milk**
**3 large tomatoes**
**25 g (1oz) butter or margarine**
**salt and pepper**

1 Toast the bread, and spread it with butter and French mustard. Cut the toast into fingers, and place half in an ovenproof dish.
2 Cover with half the grated cheese. Place the rest of the toast on top, and cover with the remaining cheese. Pour the milk evenly over the mixture.
3 Slice tomatoes and place on top. Cover and leave to stand for at least 20 minutes.
4 Preheat a moderately hot oven (190 deg C, 375 deg F, Gas 5), shelf above centre.
5 Dot the tomatoes with the butter or margarine and season with salt and pepper.
6 Bake for 40 minutes and serve immediately.

*See picture on page 58*

## TUNA TOASTS

(Serves 4)
**1 packet white sauce mix**
**250 ml (½ pint) milk**
**198 g (7oz) can tuna**
**4 large slices bread**
**paprika**

1 Make up the white sauce mix as directed, using 250 ml (½ pint) milk.
2 Preheat a hot grill
3 Carefully separate the tuna into large flakes with a fork

and add it with its oil to the prepared white sauce.
4 Toast the bread on both sides. Keep warm.
5 Re-heat the sauce gently, taking care not to break up the fish too much.
6 Place the slices of toast on 4 plates and spoon the tuna mixture over.
7 Sprinkle with paprika and serve at once.

## PICKLEBILLIES

*(Serves 4)*
**4 baps**
**butter for spreading**
**225 g (8oz) pork sausagemeat**
**125 g (4oz) streaky bacon, trimmed**
**½ level teaspoon dried mixed herbs**
**a little flour**
**25 g (1oz) dripping or cooking fat**
**mustard pickle**

1 Cut the baps almost in half and spread both sides lightly with butter.
2 Place the sausagemeat in basin. Cut the bacon into 6 mm (¼in) strips. Add to the sausagemeat with herbs; mix together with a fork.
3 Divide the mixture into 4, and using a little flour, shape the mixture into 4 round flat cakes.
4 Melt the dripping or cooking fat in a frying pan and fry the cakes on both sides—about 7 minutes each side, until cooked through.
5 Place one of the cakes inside each bap. Add a spoonful of pickle to taste and serve at once.

## CONTINENTAL SPLIT

*(Serves 6)*
**50 g (2oz) streaky bacon, trimmed and chopped**
**2 cloves garlic, crushed (optional)**
**125 g (4oz) cream cheese**
**½ level teaspoon dried mixed herbs**
**1 level tablespoon chopped parsley**
**salt and pepper**
**1 small French or Vienna loaf**
**50 g (2oz) butter**

1 Preheat a moderate oven (180 deg C, 350 deg F, Gas 4), centre shelf.
2 Place bacon in a small pan and cook until crisp. Lift from pan and drain on kitchen paper.
3 Place the crushed garlic in a small bowl with the cream cheese. Add the herbs, parsley, salt and pepper and

the pieces of bacon, and blend all well together.
4 Cut the loaf into pieces 4 cm (1½in) thick, but without cutting right through the crust, so that the slices are still attached and the base crust acts like a hinge.
5 Spread each side of the bread slices with the butter and then with the cheese mixture until all has been used up.
6 Wrap the loaf in foil and place on a baking sheet. Bake in the oven for 15-20 minutes, until the centre of the bread is heated through.
7 Roll back foil and serve at once.

## WATERCRESS SOUP

*(Serves 4)*
**1 medium-sized onion, sliced**
**25 g (1oz) butter or margarine**
**450 g (1lb) potatoes**
**2-3 bunches watercress, trimmed**
**large sprig parsley**
**250 ml (½ pint) chicken stock, or water and stock cube**
**salt and pepper**
**250 ml (½ pint) milk**
**2 tablespoons single cream or top of the milk**

1 Melt the butter or margarine in a saucepan and add the onion. Cook gently without browning until tender, stirring occasionally.
2 Peel and cube potatoes. Add to pan. Cover and cook for 10 minutes, stirring occasionally.
3 Add watercress and parsley to pan. Add the stock, or water and stock cube, and season. Cover and bring to the boil. Simmer gently for 30 minutes.
4 Rub the mixture through a fine sieve or blend in an electric blender until smooth. Pour into a clean saucepan.
5 Add the milk and the cream or top of milk and reheat until very hot, but do not boil.
6 Taste and season if necessary.

*See picture on page 59*

**Toast and Cheese Pudding,** page 56;

**TOP: Hot Sausage Salad,** see page 60                    **BELOW: Watercress Soup,** see page 57

## HOT SAUSAGE SALAD

(*Serves 4*)
**225 g (8oz) quick-cooking macaroni**
**1 tablespoon cooking oil**
**450 g (1lb) pork sausages**
**1 large onion, finely sliced**
**1 red dessert apple, cored and finely sliced**
**1 tablespoon chopped fresh parsley**
**2 tablespoons natural yogurt**
**salt and pepper**
**1 tomato, cut in wedges to garnish**

**1** Cook the macaroni in plenty of boiling water as directed on the packet. Rinse well when cooked.
**2** Meanwhile gently heat oil in a pan. Place the sausages in the pan, cook for 10-15 minutes, turning frequently until cooked. Lift sausages from the pan and slice.
**3** Place the macaroni, sliced sausages, onion, apple and parsley in a large saucepan. Add the yogurt, salt and pepper and mix well.
**4** Heat through over a low heat for 10 minutes, stirring.
**5** Arrange in a serving dish. Garnish with the tomato wedges and serve hot.

*See picture on page 59*

## CREAM OF CARROT CHOWDER WITH HOT GARLIC BREAD

(*Serves 4-6*)
**CHOWDER**
**500 g (1lb) carrots, cut lengthwise**
**1 medium-sized onion, sliced**
**550 ml (1 pint) boiling water**
**1 chicken stock cube**
**1 bay leaf**
**salt and pepper**
**198 g (7oz) can luncheon meat**
**140 g (5oz) can peas**
**2 tablespoons single cream or top milk**
**GARLIC BREAD**
**1 Vienna loaf**
**1-2 cloves garlic, crushed**
**50 g (2oz) butter**

**1** Place carrots, onion, boiling water, stock cube, bay leaf and seasoning in a saucepan. Bring to the boil, then simmer until the carrots are tender—35-40 minutes.
**2 To prepare the garlic bread:** Meanwhile slice the loaf diagonally into 2.5 cm (1in) thick slices, but do not cut

through the base crust. Blend the garlic with the softened butter. Spread on one side of each slice of bread. Push the loaf together and wrap in foil.
**3** Remove the bay leaf from the pan and rub the vegetables and liquid through a sieve, or blend in a blender, to make a purée. Chill.
**4** Just before required, preheat a moderately hot oven (190 deg C, 375 deg F, Gas 5), centre shelf.
**5** Place bread on a baking tray and bake 10 minutes.
**6** Meanwhile, dice the luncheon meat, drain the peas, and stir both into the soup with the cream or top milk.
**7** Serve the soup cold, with the hot garlic bread.

*See picture on page 58*

## CHEESY TOASTS WITH HAM

(*Serves 2-4*)
**4 small slices wholemeal bread**
**butter for spreading**
**1 egg**
**salt and pepper**
**50 g (2oz) cheese, finely grated**
**paprika**
**225g (8oz) cold cooked ham or bacon**
**2 sliced tomatoes**

**1** Preheat a moderately hot grill.
**2** Toast the bread on one side and spread the untoasted side with butter.
**3** Separate the egg yolk from the white, placing them in two bowls. Whisk the white until stiff and standing in peaks. Break the yolk and fold into the whisked white with the salt and pepper and cheese.
**4** Pile the mixture on to the four slices of toast and grill until golden brown—about 3 minutes.
**5** Sprinkle lightly with paprika. Serve immediately with cold ham and tomatoes.

## HOT SAVOURY CHEESECAKE

*(Serves 4-5)*
125 g (4oz) cream crackers, crushed
3 good pinches cayenne pepper
75 g (3oz) butter or margarine
125 g (4oz) button mushrooms, sliced
450 g (1lb) curd cheese
3 eggs, beaten
125 g (4oz) ham, chopped
salt and pepper
3 tomatoes, sliced

1 Preheat a warm oven (170 deg C, 325 deg F, Gas 3), centre shelf
2 Mix the cream crackers with cayenne pepper. Melt 50 g (2oz) of the fat, stir into the crumbs and mix well. Press into 23 cm (9in) flan ring on baking sheet or shallow ovenproof flan dish to line base.
3 Melt remaining fat in the same pan, add the mushrooms and cook for 5 minutes.
4 Beat the curd cheese and gradually beat in the eggs, add the ham and mushrooms. Season and mix well. Spoon into the biscuit flan and arrange the sliced tomatoes round the edge.
5 Bake in the oven for 45 minutes until just set. Serve hot or warm.

## CHEESE AND ANCHOVY DIP

*(Serves 4)*
2 sticks celery
4 carrots
50 g (2oz) large radishes
½ bunch spring onions
4 anchovy fillets, finely chopped
1 level tablespoon drained capers
2 teaspoons very finely chopped onion
2 tablespoons chopped chives
200 g (7oz) carton French low-fat soft cheese
salt and pepper.

1 Wash and trim the celery, carrots, radishes and spring onions. Cut into fingers and leave soaking in cold water.
2 Mash the chopped anchovies in a bowl until smooth.
3 Chop and mash the capers and add to the bowl with chopped onions and chives.
4 Gradually blend in the soft cheese and season to taste with salt and pepper. Leave the dip to stand for 1 hour to allow the flavours to blend.
5 Turn the dip into a bowl and arrange the vegetables round attractively.

## SALMON AND CUCUMBER PUFF

*(Serves 4)*
8 cm (3in) cucumber, peeled and diced
25 g (1oz) butter or margarine
25 g (1oz) plain flour
150 ml (¼ pint) milk
1 heaped teaspoon capers, chopped
212 g (7½oz) can salmon
salt and pepper
212 g (7½oz) packet frozen puff pastry, thawed
milk for brushing

1 Preheat hot oven (220 deg C, 425 deg F, Gas 7), shelf above centre.
2 Soften the cucumber in the fat, then stir in the flour. Blend in the milk, then add the capers and juice from the can of salmon. Bring to the boil, stirring continuously.
3 Flake the fish, discarding the dark skin, and stir into the sauce. Season and turn into a bowl to cool.
4 Roll out pastry to a rectangle 30 by 35 cm (12 by 14in). Cut in two lengthways, making one piece about 3 cm (1in) wider. Place narrower pastry on a baking sheet.
5 Spread the cooled fish mixture on the pastry to within 2 cm (¾in) of edge. Damp the edge and lift on the remaining pastry, press the edges together and trim neatly. Brush with milk.
6 Bake in the oven for 20-25 minutes until risen and crisp. Slide on to a wire rack to cool.

## LENTIL AND FRANKFURTER CHOWDER

*(Serves 4)*
125 g (4oz) lentils, soaked for at least 2 hours
550 ml (1 pint) chicken stock, or water and stock cube
75 g (3oz) onion, chopped
1 stick celery, sliced
1 carrot, peeled and sliced
1 bay leaf
225 g (8oz) frankfurters, sliced
225g (8oz) potato, peeled and diced
½ level teaspoon paprika
salt and pepper

1 Drain off the water from the lentils and rinse.
2 Cook the lentils in the stock with the onion, celery and carrot for 25 minutes until tender. Sieve or liquidise.
3 Return to the pan with the remaining ingredients and cook for 10 minutes until the potato is just tender.
4 Remove the bay leaf, taste and adjust seasoning.

**Turkey, Ham and Artichoke Flan,** see opposite

62

# SALADS & COLD DISHES .5

*A welcome relief on summer days and
a contrast to heavy winter meals,
salads make the most of the vitamins
and minerals in raw vegetables.
Here are delicious combinations
which, served cold, bring out
all the flavours of their ingredients*

## TURKEY, HAM
## AND ARTICHOKE FLAN

*(Serves 4-6)*
**150 g (6oz) plain flour**
**¼ level teaspoon salt**
**75 g (3oz) margarine and lard**
**cold water to mix**
**2 canned red peppers, chopped**
**4 canned artichoke hearts, drained and quartered**
**125 g (4oz) sliced ham, cut in chunks**
**175 g (6oz) cold cooked turkey, cut in chunks**
**2 eggs**
**250 ml (½ pint) milk**
**salt and pepper**
**25 g (1oz) cheese, grated**

**1** Preheat a moderately hot oven (200 deg C, 400 deg F, Gas 6), shelf above centre.
**2** Sift flour and salt into a bowl, rub in fats, until mixture resembles fine bread crumbs. Add enough cold water to make a firm dough.
**3** Roll pastry out on a lightly floured surface and use to line a 20-23 cm (8-9in) flan dish or sandwich tin. Trim edges neatly. Line the flan with greaseproof paper or foil, and baking beans, and bake blind for 15 minutes. Remove greaseproof or foil and beans, and bake for a further 5-10 minutes until cooked, then remove from oven.

**4** Arrange peppers, artichokes, ham and turkey in flan.
**5** Beat the eggs, add the milk and seasoning, and pour over the filling. Sprinkle with the cheese.
**6** Bake the flan for about 30 minutes until filling has set and top is golden. Serve with a green salad, using any remaining artichoke hearts.

*See picture opposite*

## EASY LIVER PÂTÉ

*(Serves 6)*
**250 ml (½ pint) milk**
**slice of onion**
**slice of carrot**
**1 bay leaf**
**3 peppercorns**
**225 g (8oz) streaky bacon, trimmed**
**25 g (1oz) butter or margarine**
**25 g (1oz) plain flour**
**350 g (12oz) calves' or lambs' liver**
**1 egg, lightly beaten**
**salt and pepper**

**1** Preheat a moderate oven (180 deg C, 350 deg F, Gas 4), centre shelf.
**2** Place the milk in a saucepan with the onion, carrot, bay leaf and peppercorns. Bring slowly to the boil; remove from the heat and leave to stand for 10 minutes.

3 Use half the bacon to line the base of a 15 cm (6in) soufflé or ovenproof dish.
4 Meanwhile melt the butter or margarine in a saucepan and stir in the flour. Cook for 3 minutes. Strain the milk and gradually blend in. Bring to the boil, stirring continuously, and simmer for 2 minutes.
5 Place the liver in a shallow pan and cover with cold water. Bring to the boil; simmer for 5 minutes and drain.
6 Mince the liver with the remaining bacon and stir into the sauce with the egg. Season well.
7 Pour mixture into the prepared dish and cover with a piece of greased greaseproof paper or kitchen foil. Stand the dish in a shallow pan of water and cook in the oven for 1½ hours.
8 Leave to cool in the dish then chill through— for at least 2 hours. Serve with warm toast or crisp rolls and a salad.

## HARLEQUIN SALAD

(Serves 4)
700 g (1½lb) new potatoes
4 spring onions, trimmed and finely chopped
225 g (8oz) slice of ham, diced
2 canned red peppers, cut into strips
3 rounded tablespoons thick mayonnaise
salt and pepper
lettuce
chives to garnish

1 Scrape the potatoes, place in boiling salted water, cook until tender and drain. (Or scrub, cook in their skins, and peel while still hot.) Then leave to cool. Cut the potatoes into large dice and place in a mixing bowl.
2 Add the onions, ham and peppers to the potatoes. Carefully stir in the mayonnaise. Season to taste.
3 Line a serving bowl with lettuce and spoon the salad into the centre. Sprinkle with chopped chives.

## CITRON TONGUE

(Serves 4)
small pieces of cold cooked tongue
3 tomatoes
1 clove garlic, crushed
1 tablespoon chopped parsley
3 tablespoons oil
grated rind of 1 lemon
1 tablespoon lemon juice
salt and pepper

1 Arrange the pieces of cold tongue in a dish.

2 To skin the tomatoes: place in a bowl and cover with boiling water for ½ minute, drain and cover with cold water, then strip off skins. Chop finely; place in bowl.
3 Add the garlic, parsley, oil, lemon rind and lemon juice. Season and mix well.
4 Pour this marinade over the tongue and cover the dish. Leave to soak for at least 3 hours, or overnight, in a cool place or in the refrigerator.
5 Serve in the marinade.

## HERBY BEEF LOAF

(Serves 6)
700 g (1½lb) chuck steak
175 g (6oz) back bacon
4 slices white bread
¼ level teaspoon dried mixed herbs
1½ level tablespoons chopped parsley
2 eggs, beaten
salt and pepper

1 Preheat a moderately hot oven (190 deg C, 375 deg F, Gas 5), centre shelf. Grease a 1 kg (2lb) loaf tin.
2 Remove any excess fat from the steak and bacon, including bacon rinds. Cut steak into pieces and mince with the bacon and bread into a mixing bowl.
3 Add the herbs, parsley and eggs and season well. Mix all ingredients well and pack into the loaf tin.
4 Smooth the surface and cover the tin with a piece of buttered greaseproof paper. Bake for 1¼ hours.
5 Remove and leave to cool in the tin. Then chill through—about 3 hours. Turn out carefully on to a serving dish. Slice and serve with salads.

## ROLLED HAM SALAD

(Serves 2-4)
225 g (8oz) frozen mixed vegetable
4 level tablespoons thick mayonnaise
salt and pepper
4 slices honey roast ham
salad to garnish

1 Cook the mixed vegetables in a small saucepan of boiling water as directed. Drain and leave to cool.
2 Place the mayonnaise in a small bowl and add the cold vegetables. Mix well and season to taste.
3 Spoon on to the slices of ham, dividing equally between them and roll up. Arrange on plates and garnish with some salad.
Note: If liked, add a chopped hard-boiled egg to the filling before rolling up in the ham.

## PORK AND ORANGE SALAD

(Serves 4)
2 oranges
350 g (12oz) cooked pork, diced
50 g (2oz) cashew nuts
2 sticks celery, sliced
1 lettuce
a few sprigs of endive or watercress
DRESSING
2 tablespoons oil
1 tablespoon lemon juice
salt and pepper

1 Cut the peel and pith from the oranges with a very sharp knife. Cut out the segments between the membranes and place in a bowl.
2 Add the pork, cashew nuts and celery to the orange.
3 **To make the dressing:** Mix the oil, lemon juice and seasoning in a cup, beat lightly with a fork and pour over the pork mixture. Toss well. Leave to stand for at least 30 minutes in a cool place.
4 Wash, drain and dry the lettuce. Arrange a few leaves round the edge of a salad bowl or on a plate. Spoon the pork mixture into the centre. Garnish with a few sprigs of endive or watercress.
5 Place the remaining lettuce in another bowl and serve separately.

## MINTED LAMB SALAD

(Serves 4)
700 g (1½lb) new potatoes
225 g (8oz) frozen peas
350 g (12oz) cooked lamb, chopped
4 tomatoes, cut in wedges
DRESSING
2 rounded teaspoons concentrated mint sauce
3 tablespoons oil
1 tablespoon vinegar
1 rounded tablespoon chopped chives
salt and pepper

1 Scrape the potatoes, place in boiling salted water, cook until tender and drain. (Or scrub, cook in their skins, and peel while still hot.) Then dice while still hot and place in a large bowl.
2 Cook the peas as directed on the packet, then drain and add to the potatoes with the lamb.
3 **To make the dressing:** Mix the mint sauce, oil, vinegar, chives and seasoning together in a small bowl. Pour over

the potato mixture while the potatoes are still warm. Mix thoroughly to coat all ingredients and leave to cool.
4 Pile the salad in the centre of a serving dish and arrange the tomatoes round the edge.
**Note:** The flavours of this dish improve with standing.

## CHICKEN JUMBLE

(Serves 3-4)
75 g (3oz) long-grain rice
175 g (6oz) frozen peas
175 g (6oz) frozen sweetcorn
225 g (8oz) cooked chicken
½ cucumber, peeled and diced
25 g (1oz) shelled walnuts, chopped
lettuce to garnish
DRESSING
2 tablespoons oil
1 tablespoon vinegar
1 tablespoon lemon juice
¼ level teaspoon mustard
¼ level teaspoon salt
large pinch pepper
1 clove garlic, crushed (optional)

1 Cook the rice in plenty of boiling salted water for about 12 minutes, or until tender. Drain and rinse. Leave to cool.
2 Cook the peas and sweetcorn as directed on the packets. Leave to cool.
3 Tear the chicken into bite-sized pieces.
4 **To make the dressing:** In a large serving bowl, stir together all the dressing ingredients.
5 Mix in the cold rice, peas, sweetcorn, chicken, cucumber and walnuts.
6 Stir gently until thoroughly coated with dressing. Garnish with lettuce.

**Chicken and Ham Galantine,** see page 69

**Summer Salad,** see page 68

## GAMMON MOUSSE

*(Serves 4)*
**150 ml (¼ pint) very hot water or chicken stock**
**1 envelope gelatine**
**225 g (8oz) cooked gammon**
**pepper**
**150 ml (5fl oz) double cream**
**2 egg whites**
**chopped parsley to garnish**

**1** Pour hot water or stock into a small bowl. Sprinkle on the gelatine and leave to soak in hot water to dissolve the gelatine. Then leave to cool.
**2** Finely chop the gammon, then pound to a paste with the end of a rolling pin, or use a pestle and mortar. Season the gammon with pepper. Unless meat is very mild it will not need salt.
**3** Stir the cooled gelatine into the gammon paste and mix together well.
**4** Whisk the cream until it is light and frothy and just holding its shape. Fold cream into the gammon mixture and leave in a cool place until just beginning to set.
**5** Place the egg whites in a bowl and beat until stiff and standing in peaks. Fold into the gammon mixture and turn into soufflé dish. Chill for 1 hour or longer, until set.
**6** Sprinkle the surface with parsley and serve cold.

## ICED TOMATO RING

*(Serves 6)*
**396 g (14oz) can tomatoes**
**25 g (1oz) grated onion**
**1 level teaspoon very finely chopped fresh thyme or**
**¼ level teaspoon dried thyme**
**1 teaspoon tomato purée**
**1 clove garlic, crushed**
**1 level tablespoon castor sugar**
**½ level teaspoon salt**
**finely grated rind and juice ½ lemon**
**1 small green pepper, de-seeded and finely chopped (optional)**
**275 ml (½ pint) well flavoured stock (made with water and 1 stock cube)**
**freshly ground black pepper**
**¼ cucumber, thinly sliced**
**1 bunch watercress, to garnish**
**5 gherkins, sliced into fans, to garnish**

**1** Press the canned tomatoes and juice through a fine sieve with the onion and thyme, and tomato purée.

**2** Add the crushed garlic, sugar, salt, lemon rind and juice, green pepper, if using, and stock. Mix well.
**3** Season well with freshly ground black pepper and more salt, then turn into a plastic container and freeze until firm round edges—about 1 hour.
**4** Mash the firm water ice until slushy, then freeze again until firm round edges.
**5** Mash the firm ice smoothly then turn it into an 825 ml (1½ pint) ring mould and freeze until firm.
**6** Turn the ice out of the container about ¾ hour before serving on to a plate decorated with cucumber. Garnish with watercress and gherkins and refrigerate.
**Note:** For a main meal, try filling with cottage cheese mixed with salad cream, chopped celery and chives—or, best of all, prawns mixed with mayonnaise.

## SUMMER SALAD

*(Serves 3-4)*
**1 lettuce**
**225 g (8oz) cooked ham, cut into strips**
**2 tomatoes, sliced**
**1 green pepper, de-seeded and cut into strips**
**1 red pepper, de-seeded and cut into strips**
**½ cucumber, peeled and sliced**
**bunch of radishes, trimmed and sliced**
**2 hard-boiled eggs, quartered**
**DRESSING**
**a pinch each of salt, pepper, dry mustard and castor sugar**
**6 tablespoons corn oil**
**3 tablespoons wine vinegar**
**a few drops of Worcestershire sauce**

**1** Wash and dry the lettuce and tear into pieces.
**2** Arrange the ham, tomatoes, peppers, cucumber, radishes and hard-boiled eggs in a salad bowl.
**3 To make the dressing:** Place the seasonings in a small basin and gradually stir in the oil, vinegar and Worcestershire sauce.
**4** Pour the dressing over the salad and serve at once.

*See picture on page 67*

## CANARY ISLAND SALAD

*(Serves 4)*
75 g (3oz) long-grain rice
175 g (6oz) sliced cooked ham, diced
50 g (2oz) button mushrooms, halved or quartered
25 g (1oz) salted peanuts
2 bananas
lettuce
**DRESSING**
4 tablespoons oil
2 tablespoons vinegar
salt and pepper
¼ level teaspoon dry mustard
¼ level teaspoon castor sugar
1 level tablespoon chopped chives

**1** Cook the rice in plenty of boiling salted water until just tender—about 12 minutes. Drain, rinse with cold water, and allow to cool.
**2 To make the dressing:** Blend together the oil, vinegar, salt, pepper, mustard, sugar and chives.
**3** Mix together in a bowl the cold rice, diced ham, raw mushrooms and peanuts
**4** Peel and slice the bananas and add to the bowl with the dressing. Toss well and serve with lettuce.

*See picture on page 58*

## KIPPER SALAD

*(Serves 1)*
½ level teaspoon made mustard
½ level teaspoon castor sugar
1 tablespoon oil
2 teaspoons vinegar
pepper
1 whole kipper
2 level tablespoons chopped watercress
2 sticks celery, finely sliced
½ eating apple

**1** In a basin, blend together the mustard, sugar, oil, vinegar and pepper.
**2** Loosen and remove the central bone from the kipper, then run the point of a sharp knife under the little bones down the length of the fish. Lift them away, leaving two fillets. Gently pull away the skin from the fillets.
**3** Using scissors, cut fillets across into thin strips.
**4** Stir the fish into the dressing, and add the watercress and celery.
**5** Remove the core and cut the apple into small dice. Add

to the other ingredients in the basin.
**6** Mix everything well in to the dressing and leave to stand for 15 minutes to allow the flavours to blend.

## CHICKEN AND HAM GALANTINE

*(Serves 6-8)*
1½ kg (3¼lb) boiling chicken
1 small onion, peeled and quartered
1 small carrot, peeled and sliced
1 small bay leaf
1 bouquet garni
salt and pepper
2 level teaspoons powdered gelatine
40 g (1½oz) parsley, finely chopped
350 g (12oz) cooked ham, finely chopped
125 g (4oz) cooked tongue, finely chopped
a few chives
2 radishes, sliced
a few sprigs parsley

**1** Place the chicken in a saucepan and pour in about 5 cm (2in) depth of water. Add the vegetables, bay leaf, bouquet garni, salt and pepper. Cover and cook very gently for about 1 hour until the chicken is tender.
**2** When cooked, transfer the chicken to a plate, skim off the fat from the stock and strain. (If possible, leave overnight to allow the fat to harden, then scrape off.)
**3** Measure 575 ml (1 pint) of the stock into a jug making up with water if necessary. Place the gelatine in a small bowl in a pan of hot water, pour over a little stock and stir until dissolved. Then stir into the measured stock.
**4** When chicken has cooled, remove the meat from the bones. Leave the breast pieces in long narrow pieces and finely chop remaining chicken.
**5** Place half of the chopped chicken evenly in the base of a 750 g (1½lb) loaf tin.
**6** Cut the breast pieces of meat into long narrow strips, dip 4 of them in a little of the jelly, roll in the chopped parsley and arrange lengthways on the chopped chicken. Press down lightly.
**7** Spread on half the chopped ham and pour over a little of the jelly, to just fill in. (Too much will cause the chopped parsley to float.)
**8** Place the chopped tongue along the centre of the tin, cover with the remaining chopped ham.
**9** Pour over a little more of the jelly, press the meats down to firm, and put in the refrigerator for half an hour to set.
**10** Dip 4 more strips of chicken in jelly and parsley and arrange over, cover with remaining chopped chicken.
**11** Pour in the chicken jelly, reserving some for the decoration, and allow to set in the refrigerator.
**12** To serve, turn out of tin, brush with chicken jelly and decorate with chives, radish slices and parsley.
**Note:** If you have the time, set the layers in the refrigerator after every other stage.

*See picture on page 66*

**Orange Cheese Pancakes,** see opposite

# HOT PUDDINGS

*Here are the hot favourites—as popular as ever, but tailored to your time. These recipes can help you to serve a warming end to a meal or an impressive finale when you are entertaining*

35  25

## ORANGE CHEESE PANCAKES

*(Serves 4)*
**125 g (4oz) plain flour**
**pinch of salt**
**1 egg**
**250 ml (½ pint) milk**
**about 2 tablespoons oil**
**FILLING**
**two 85 g (3oz) packets full fat soft cheese**
**finely grated rind of 1 medium-sized orange**
**1 tablespoon milk**
**1 level tablespoon castor sugar**
**ORANGE SAUCE**
**250 ml (½ pint) orange juice**
**1 level tablespoon arrowroot**
**3 level tablespoons sugar**
**rind peeled from 1 orange**
**1 level tablespoon flaked almonds**

1 Sift the flour and salt into a bowl and make a hollow in the centre. Add the egg and a little of the milk.
2 Beat the mixture, gradually mixing in the flour and adding more milk, to make a smooth batter
3 Stir in the remaining milk and 1 tablespoon oil. Cover and keep aside for 30 minutes.
4 **To make the filling:** Meanwhile, place cheese, orange rind, milk and castor sugar in a bowl and cream together.
5 Heat a little oil in an 18 cm (7in) frying pan. When really hot, pour in enough batter to just coat the base. Cook

until underside is golden, then turn and cook until the second side is golden.
6 Tip on to a plate and keep hot. Cook remaining pancakes.
7 Divide the filling between the pancakes. Roll up and place in a hot, shallow ovenproof dish. Keep warm.
8 **To make orange sauce:** Blend the orange juice into the arrowroot in a saucepan, add the sugar, and stir while bringing to the boil. Cook for 1 minute. Meanwhile finely shred the orange rind and cook in a little water for 2 minutes. Drain and add to sauce with flaked almonds.
9 Pour the sauce over the pancakes and serve hot.
**Note:** These may be prepared to end of stage 9, then covered and kept warm in the oven.

*See picture opposite*

20  35

## HOT MOCHA SOUFFLÉ

*(Serves 4-6)*
**150 ml (¼ pint) milk**
**2 level teaspoons instant coffee**
**25 g (1oz) plain chocolate**
**25 g (1oz) butter or margarine**
**25 g (1oz) plain flour**
**50 g (2oz) castor sugar**
**a few drops vanilla essence**
**3 large eggs**

1 Preheat a moderately hot oven (190 deg C, 375 deg F, Gas 5), centre shelf. Butter a 15 cm (6in) soufflé dish and

tie a double band of greased greaseproof paper round the outside to stand 5 cm (2in) above the rim. Alternatively, use a 1 litre (2 pint) ovenproof dish.

**2** Place the milk together with the coffee and the chocolate in a small saucepan and heat gently until the chocolate has completely melted.

**3** Melt the butter or margarine in a saucepan and stir in the flour. Cook for 1 minute, stirring. Gradually blend in the milk mixture and bring to the boil. Stir until the mixture thickens and falls away from the sides of the pan.

**4** Remove from heat; beat in sugar and vanilla essence.

**5** Separate the egg yolks from the whites, placing the whites in a clean bowl for beating, and stirring the yolks into the chocolate mixture.

**6** Whisk the egg whites until they are stiff and standing in peaks. Fold the egg whites into chocolate mixture carefully and lightly, using a metal spoon, until evenly mixed.

**7** Turn into the prepared dish and bake for 35 minutes until well risen.

**8** Serve hot with vanilla ice-cream or single cream.

# BILBERRY CRUNCH

*(Serves 4)*
**482 g (1lb 1oz) jar bilberries in syrup**
**2 level tablespoons cornflour**
**sugar to taste (optional)**
**75 g (3oz) plain flour**
**50 g (2oz) butter**
**1 level tablespoon rolled oats**
**2 level tablespoons peanuts or walnuts, finely chopped**
**2 level tablespoons demerara sugar**

**1** Preheat a moderate oven (180 deg C, 350 deg F, Gas 4), shelf towards top.

**2** Strain bilberry syrup into a saucepan and blend in the cornflour. Bring to boil, stirring, cook 2 minutes. Add bilberries, and sugar if liked. Turn into ovenproof dish.

**3** Place the flour in a mixing bowl. Add butter to flour and rub in until mixture resembles breadcrumbs.

**4** Add the rolled oats, chopped nuts and demerara sugar. Mix the ingredients well and spread over the pie filling.

**5** Bake about 30 minutes until top is lightly browned.

# RICH RAISIN PUDDING WITH ORANGE SAUCE

*(Serves 4-6)*
**125 g (4oz) butter and margarine**
**125 g (4oz) castor sugar**
**2 eggs**
**grated rind of 1 orange**
**125 g (4oz) self-raising flour**
**50 g (2oz) stoned raisins**
**ORANGE SAUCE**
**50 g (2oz) castor sugar**
**150 ml (¼ pint) water**
**2 large oranges**
**3 level teaspoons cornflour**

**1** Prepare a steamer and put on to heat.

**2** Grease a 1 litre (1½ pint) pudding basin and a double layer of greaseproof paper for top.

**3** Cream the butter or margarine and sugar together with a wooden spoon until light and fluffy.

**4** Beat in the eggs one at a time, beating well after each addition. Fold in the grated orange rind, flour and raisins.

**5** Spoon the mixture into the prepared basin and lay the paper on top, twisting the edges securely under the rim of the bowl.

**6** Place in the top of the steamer and cover. Steam for 2-2¼ hours, adding more boiling water to the steamer when necessary.

**7 To make orange sauce:** Place the sugar and water in a saucepan and heat gently until sugar has dissolved.

**8** Thinly peel some of the rind from one orange and cut into narrow strips. Add to the hot syrup and simmer for 5-6 minutes until tender.

**9** Squeeze the juice from both oranges and blend with the cornflour. Stir into the boiling syrup; simmer for 2 minutes until clear and slightly thickened. Turn the pudding on to a serving dish. Serve hot sauce separately.

# FRUMALLOW FLAN

*(Serves 4-5)*
**1 baked pastry flan case, about 15-18 cm (6-7in)**
**4 tablespoons apricot jam**
**juice of ½ lemon**
**2 medium-sized bananas**
**about 18 marshmallows**

**1** Place the flan case on an ovenproof plate. Spread the base of the flan with apricot jam.

**2** Peel bananas and cut into 1 cm (½in) slices. Toss in

lemon juice to coat. Then arrange the flan, pressing the banana into the jam to make a level surface.

**3** Preheat a moderately hot grill.

**4** Cut the marshmallows in half and arrange with the cut side down all over the flan, alternating pink and white if not all one colour.

**5** Place the plate under the grill and grill till golden—about 2-3 minutes.

**6** Serve immediately.

## TUTTI-FRUTTI FLAN

*(Serves 4-6)*
1 baked pastry flan case about 15-18 cm (6-7in)
75 g (3oz) glacé cherries, finely chopped
50 g (2oz) chopped mixed peel
15 g (½oz) angelica, finely chopped
1 egg, whisked
50 g (2oz) unsalted butter
50 g (2oz) castor sugar

**1** Preheat a moderate oven (180 deg C, 350 deg F, Gas 4), centre shelf.

**2** Place the flan case on a baking sheet or ovenproof plate.

**3** Mix together the glacé cherries, mixed peel and angelica and spread them over the base of the flan case.

**4** Mix the egg, butter and sugar in a small saucepan. Bring to the boil, stirring continuously, and pour over the glacé fruits in the flan case.

**5** Bake for 25 minutes until the mixture is set. Can also be served cold.

## CRISPY APPLE CHARLOTTE

*(Serves 4-6)*
4 heaped tablespoons demerara sugar
1 level teaspoon ground cinnamon
5 thin slices white bread
125 g (4oz) butter or margarine
450 g (1lb) cooking apples

**1** Preheat a moderately hot oven (200 deg C, 400 deg F, Gas 6), shelf above centre. Thickly butter a 1 litre (1½ -2 pint) ovenproof dish.

**2** Mix the sugar and cinnamon together, and sprinkle some of this mixture over the sides and base of the buttered dish.

**3** Remove the crusts and cut the bread into triangles.

**4** Melt the butter or margarine in a small saucepan, and then remove from the heat. Dip each piece of bread quickly into the melted butter and line the base and sides

of the dish, reserving sufficient bread to cover the top.

**5** Peel, core and slice the apples.

**6** Layer the apples and sugar in the dish, keeping a little sugar for the top. Cover the apples with the remaining dipped bread and sprinkle with the rest of the sugar.

**7** Bake for 45 minutes until the surface is crisp and golden and the apples tender.

**8** Serve hot with lightly whipped cream.

## APPLE SOUFFLE OMELETTE

*(Serves 2)*
**FILLING**
25 g (1oz) butter
1 heaped tablespoon apricot jam
1 large cooking apple
25 g (1oz) castor sugar
**SOUFFLE OMELETTE**
2 eggs
25 g (1oz) castor sugar
1 level teaspoon cornflour
¼ teaspoon vanilla essence

**1 To make the filling:** Place the butter and jam in a small saucepan and heat very gently until melted.

**2** Meanwhile, peel, core and slice the apple and add to the pan. Cover and heat very gently for about 10 minutes shaking the saucepan occasionally, until the apple slices are soft but not pulpy. Add the castor sugar to sweeten the apple and keep hot.

**3 To make the soufflé omelette:** Separate the egg yolks from the whites and place in separate bowls.

**4** Add the castor sugar, cornflour and vanilla essence to the yolks. Cream together until thick and pale.

**5** Whisk the egg whites until stiff and standing in peaks. Carefully fold the whites into the egg yolk mixture using a metal spoon.

**6** Preheat a hot grill.

**7** Lightly butter a heavy 25 cm (10in) frying pan. Heat gently. When hot pour the egg mixture into the frying pan and level the surface. Cook slowly until the underside is just brown and sides are setting.

**8** Place under the hot grill until the top is golden.

**9** Make a slit across the centre with a knife, spoon the filling on to one half and fold omelette over.

**10** Slide on to a plate, sprinkle with a little extra castor sugar, and serve at once.

# TREACLE TART

(Serves 4-6)
**SHORTCRUST PASTRY**
**150 g (6oz) plain flour**
**pinch of salt**
**75 g (3oz) butter or margarine**
**cold water to mix**
**FILLING**
**3 rounded tablespoons golden syrup**
**1 rounded tablespoon black treacle**
**1 lemon**
**large pinch ground ginger**
**50 g (2oz) fresh white breadcrumbs**

1 Preheat a hot oven (220 deg C, 425 deg F, Gas 7), shelf above centre.
2 **To make pastry:** Sift the flour and salt into a mixing bowl and add the butter or margarine. Rub in, until the mixture resembles fine breadcrumbs. Mix to a firm dough with a little cold water.
3 Form into a ball, roll out on a lightly-floured surface and use to line a 23-25 cm (9-10in) ovenproof plate. Trim pastry, keeping the trimmings, and flute the edges in a decorative pattern.
4 **To make the filling:** Place the syrup and treacle in a small saucepan and warm gently for a few minutes.
5 Finely grate the lemon rind and squeeze out 1 tablespoon juice. Then add both to the syrup with the ginger and breadcrumbs.
6 Spread the mixture over the pastry to within 2.5 cm (1in) of the edge.
7 Roll out the pastry trimmings and cut into ½ cm (¼in) strips. Damp the ends of each strip with water and lay the strips in a lattice pattern over the tart.
8 Bake for 15-20 minutes until pastry is golden brown. Serve hot with single cream. (Can also be served cold.)

# MINCEMEAT BREAD AND BUTTER PUDDING

(Serves 2)
**75 g (3oz) bread, preferably French loaf**
**butter for spreading**
**3-4 level tablespoons mincemeat**
**2 eggs**
**milk**
**1-2 tablespoons demerara sugar**

1 Preheat a moderate oven (180 deg C, 350 deg F, Gas 4), centre shelf.
2 Slice the bread and spread with butter. Cut into pieces to fit a 550 ml (1 pint) ovenproof dish.
3 Arrange half the buttered bread in the dish, butter side down. Spread the mincemeat over it and cover with the remainder of the bread, butter side up.
4 Beat the eggs, and make up to 250 ml (½ pint) with milk.
5 Pour over the bread and sprinkle the demerara sugar over the top.
6 Bake for 30 minutes, until set and golden on top. Serve with thickly whipped cream.
**Note:** Jam or marmalade can be used instead of mincemeat to vary the flavour. Alternatively, try adding a layer of apple slices and finely chopped dates.

*See picture opposite*

**Mincemeat Bread and Butter Pudding,** see opposite

## ORANGE COCONUT CRUMB

*(Serves 4)*
75 g (3oz) butter or margarine
3 large oranges
125 g (4oz) white breadcrumbs
50 g (2oz) desiccated coconut
3 level tablespoons clear honey
juice of 1 lemon
1 tablespoon cointreau (optional)

1 Preheat a warm oven (170 deg C, 325 deg F, Gas 3), shelf towards top. Grease a medium-sized, shallow ovenproof dish with a little of the butter or margarine.
2 Cut the peel and pith from the oranges with a very sharp knife. Cut out the segments of the orange between the membrane with a sharp knife.
3 Melt the rest of the butter or margarine in a frying pan. Add the breadcrumbs and coconut to the butter and stir until the fat is absorbed.
4 Use half the crumbs to coat the base and sides of the dish. Place the orange segments in the dish and cover with the remaining crumbs.
5 Put the honey, lemon and cointreau (if using) into a small saucepan. Heat gently and stir till well blended.
6 Pour the mixture over the crumbs in the dish.
7 Bake for 30 minutes until crisp and golden. (Can be served cold.)

## GOLDEN CHEESECAKE

*(Serves 4-6)*
**SHORTCRUST PASTRY**
150 g (6oz) plain flour
pinch of salt
75 g (3oz) butter or margarine
cold water to mix
**FILLING**
225 g (8oz) cottage cheese
40 g (1½oz) castor sugar
1 tablespoon golden syrup
25 g (1oz) butter or margarine
1 egg, beaten
grated rind of 1 lemon
2 teaspoons lemon juice
pinch of grated nutmeg
25 g (1oz) currants

1 Preheat a moderately hot oven (190 deg C, 375 deg F, Gas 5), shelf above centre. Place an 18 cm (7in) flan ring on a baking sheet, or use a sandwich tin.

2 **To make the pastry:** Sift the flour and salt into a bowl, and add the butter or margarine. Rub in with the fingertips until the mixture resembles fine breadcrumbs. Mix to a firm dough with a little cold water.
3 Form into a ball and roll out on a lightly floured surface and use to line the flan ring or sandwich tin.
4 Trim the edges and pinch to make a decorative edge.
5 **To make the filling:** Sieve the cottage cheese into a bowl and add the sugar and syrup.
6 Melt the butter or margarine in a saucepan, mix in the egg and stir into the cheese mixture with the lemon rind and juice, nutmeg and currants.
7 Pour this mixture into the pastry case and bake in the oven for 30-35 minutes until pale golden brown and firm. (Can also be served cold.)

## APPLE SURPRISE

*(Serves 4-6)*
250 ml (½ pint) milk
40 g (1½oz) semolina
125 g (4oz) soft margarine
125 g (4oz) castor sugar
3 eggs, separated
75 g (3oz) seedless raisins
1 level teaspoon ground cinnamon
50 g (2oz) flaked almonds
225 g (8oz) dessert apples, preferably Cox's Orange
  Pippins, peeled and coarsely chopped

1 Preheat a moderate oven (150 deg C, 350 deg F, Gas 4), centre shelf. Well grease a 28 by 18 cm (11 by 7in) ovenproof dish.
2 Heat the milk in a small saucepan and sprinkle in the semolina, stirring continuously. Cook until the mixture thickens, still stirring, then reduce heat and cook for a further 3 minutes.
3 Cover with damp greaseproof paper to prevent skin forming; allow to cool.
4 Meanwhile, in a medium-sized mixing bowl, cream the margarine and sugar until light and fluffy. Beat in the egg yolks. Add the raisins, cinnamon, almonds, apples and cooled semolina.
5 Whisk the egg whites until stiff and standing in peaks. Fold into the mixture.
6 Transfer into the greased dish and bake for 1 hour until springy to the touch.
7 Serve hot with cream. (Can also be served cold.)

## SWEET TOPSY

*(Serves 4-6)*
**7 tablespoons clear honey**
**8 glacé cherries**
**25 g (1oz) seeded raisins**
**25 g (1oz) sultanas**
**25 g (1oz) mixed peel**
**125 g (4oz) butter**
**125 g (4oz) castor sugar**
**2 eggs, whisked**
**125 g (4oz) self-raising flour**
**grated rind and juice of 1 lemon**
**1 tablespoon milk**
**2 level teaspoons arrowroot**
**1 tablespoon water**

**1** Preheat a moderately hot oven (190 deg C, 375 deg F, Gas 5), centre shelf. Lightly oil a square 15 cm (6in) cake tin.
**2** Spread 3 tablespoons of the honey over the base of the cake tin.
**3** Halve the cherries and arrange in a square in one corner. Repeat with the raisins, sultanas and then the mixed peel, so that the four squares are filled.
**4** Place the butter and sugar in a mixing bowl and beat together until light and fluffy. Gradually beat in the 2 eggs, beating well after each addition. Sieve the flour into the bowl and gradually fold it into the egg mixture with the lemon rind. If necessary, fold in 1 tablespoon of milk to make a soft dropping consistency.
**5** Turn the mixture into the cake tin and smooth the top.
**6** Bake for 45 minutes, until the pudding is golden brown and springy to the touch.
**7** Remove from the oven and leave to stand while making the sauce.
**8** Strain the lemon juice into a saucepan with the remaining honey. Heat gently until honey has dissolved.
**9** Blend the arrowroot with the water and pour into the pan. Bring to the boil, stirring continuously, and cook until thickened—about 2 minutes.
**10** Turn the pudding on to a hot serving dish and pour the sauce over.

## LEMON PUDDING

*(Serves 4-5)*
**75 g (3oz) butter**
**150 g (5oz) castor sugar**
**3 large eggs, separated**
**grated rind and juice of 1 lemon**
**100 g (4oz) plain flour, sieved**
**275 ml (½ pint) milk**

**1** Preheat a moderately hot oven (190 deg C, 375 deg F, Gas 5), centre shelf. Lightly butter a 1 litre (2 pint) pie or ovenproof soufflé dish.
**2** Cream together the butter and sugar, beat in the yolks, lemon rind and juice.
**3** Fold in the flour then gradually blend in the milk.
**4** Whisk the egg whites until stiff and standing in peaks, then carefully fold into the soufflé mixture using a large metal spoon. Pour into the dish.
**5** Bake for about 35-40 minutes until well risen and lightly browned.

## QUEEN'S APRICOT MERINGUE

*(Serves 4)*
**25 g (1oz) butter**
**4 slices from large thin-sliced loaf, crusts removed**
**75 g (3oz) castor sugar**
**½ level teaspoon ground cinnamon**
**411 g (14½oz) can apricot halves, well drained**
**3 eggs**
**400 ml (14fl oz) milk, warmed**

**1** Spread the bread with the butter and then cut into squares. Use half the bread to line an ovenproof dish, placing it buttered side down.
**2** Mix together 25 g (1oz) sugar and cinnamon, sprinkle half on to the bread in the dish. Arrange the apricot halves on top then cover with the remaining bread. Sprinkle with remaining sugar mixture.
**3** Separate 2 eggs and beat the yolks with the remaining whole egg. Stir in milk and pour over bread in the dish.
**4** Leave to stand while preheating a moderate oven (180 deg C, 350 deg F, Gas 4), centre shelf.
**5** Bake in the oven for 35-45 minutes until just set—time depends on depth of dish. Then remove and reduce oven temperature to lowest setting.
**6** Whisk egg whites until stiff and standing in peaks, then whisk in remaining 50 g (2oz) sugar. Spread lightly on the pudding to cover it completely. Return to the oven and bake for 20-30 minutes until meringue is set and lightly brown. Serve immediately.

**Spiced Plum Tart,** see opposite

# COOL DESSERTS 7

*Delicious concoctions of fruit and cream, meringues and jellies are ideal for summer days, and children love them. And for elaborate dinner parties a cold dessert can make a light conclusion to the meal*

## SPICED PLUM TART

*(Serves 4)*
100 g (4oz) plain flour
100 g (4oz) butter
75 g (3oz) ground almonds
½ level teaspoon mixed spice
¼ level teaspoon finely grated lemon rind
100 g (4oz) castor sugar
1 egg yolk
about 700 g (1½lb) plums, stoned
4 rounded tablespoons apricot jam
2 tablespoons lemon juice
15 g (½oz) flaked almonds

1 Place the flour in a mixing bowl, add the butter and rub in until the mixture resembles breadcrumbs. Stir in 50 g (2oz) of the ground almonds, the mixed spice, lemon rind and half the sugar.
2 Stir in the egg yolk to make a stiff dough. Knead lightly till smooth. Then place in a polythene bag and chill for 1 hour until firm.
3 Roll out the dough on a lightly floured surface and press into a 23 cm (9in) fluted flan dish, or flan ring set on a baking sheet. Chill well for at least 1 hour.
4 Preheat a moderate oven (180 deg C, 350 deg F, Gas 4), centre shelf.
5 Mix the remaining ground almonds and sugar together, and sprinkle over base of the flan. Arrange the plums on top of this mixture.
6 Bake for 30-35 minutes until golden brown.

7 Heat jam and lemon juice till very hot then rub through a sieve. Spoon the glaze over the plums. Sprinkle with flaked almonds. Allow to cool, then chill.
8 Serve cold with cream.

*See picture opposite*

## ALICE'S ORANGE CREAM

*(Serves 4)*
2 small oranges
1 envelope gelatine
4 tablespoons water
400 ml (¾ pint) milk
3 egg yolks
50 g (2oz) castor sugar
150 ml (5fl oz) double cream
milk chocolate flake, or grated plain chocolate

1 Finely grate the rind from the oranges.
2 Place the gelatine in a small bowl with the water and allow to swell. Place the bowl in a pan of hot water and allow the gelatine to melt.
3 Gently heat the milk in a saucepan with the grated orange rind, until almost boiling. Remove from heat.
4 Beat the egg yolks with the sugar in a bowl and gradually stir in the milk, mix well. Pour custard into a bowl, rinse the pan with cold water, and return custard to the pan. (Use a double saucepan if you have one.)
5 Cook very gently until the custard thickens and just coats the back of the wooden spoon. Do not allow to boil.
6 Strain both the custard and gelatine into a bowl. Stand

the bowl in ice-cold water until the custard is just on the point of setting.

7 Whip 2 tablespoons of the cream in a small bowl until softly stiff. Fold into the custard mixture.

8 Wet a 15 cm (6in) round cake tin with cold water and pour in the custard mixture.

9 Chill for at least 90 minutes, and decorate when needed.

10 **To serve:** Quickly dip the tin in warm water and turn out on to a serving plate.

11 Whisk rest of cream until softly stiff. Spread over the orange cream. Sprinkle the milk chocolate flake, or grated plain chocolate, over the cream.

12 Cut the peel and pith from the oranges with a very sharp knife. Then cut out the segments between the membranes.

13 Arrange the orange segments on the cream and serve.

## SUNSHINE JELLY WHIP

*(Serves 4-5)*

**312 g (11oz) can mandarin oranges**
**1 packet orange-flavoured jelly**
**1 small can evaporated milk**
**25 g (1oz) glacé cherries, quartered**

1 Strain the juice from the mandarin oranges into a small saucepan. Break the jelly into pieces and add to the pan.

2 Heat gently until the jelly has dissolved. Pour into a measuring jug and make up to 250 ml (½ pint) with cold water.

3 Cool the jug in a bowl of ice-cold water, until the jelly is just starting to set around the edges.

4 Whisk the evaporated milk with a rotary beater until doubled in volume and the whisk leaves a trail when it is lifted.

5 Pour the jelly into a bowl and beat with the rotary beater until thick and frothy.

6 Add the evaporated milk with the cherries and most of

the mandarin oranges. Mix together and transfer to a glass serving bowl.

7 Decorate with the remaining mandarin segments.

## ORANGE FLUFF

*(Serves 4-6)*

**1 envelope gelatine**
**150 ml (¼ pint) water**
**2-3 level tablespoons castor sugar**
**178 ml (6¼oz) can frozen concentrated**
 **orange juice, thawed**
**2 egg whites**
**chocolate vermicelli to decorate**

1 Place the gelatine in a small bowl with the water and allow to swell. Then place the bowl in a pan of hot water and allow the gelatine to melt. Stir in the sugar until it has dissolved.

3 Then mix into the thawed orange juice in a mixing bowl.

4 Place the egg whites in a separate bowl and whisk until stiff and standing in peaks.

5 Whisk the orange jelly until light and frothy and just beginning to set. Quickly fold in the egg whites using a metal spoon.

6 Pour the mixture into individual serving glasses, or into one large glass bowl, and chill to set in a refrigerator. Decorate with the chocolate vermicelli.

7 Serve chilled with some small sweet biscuits.

## FRUITY APPLE FOAM

*(Serves 4)*

**225 g (8oz) cooking apples, peeled, cored and sliced**
**1-2 tablespoons clear honey**
**1 large egg, separated**
**50 g (2oz) sultanas**
**1 level tablespoon castor sugar**
**25 g (1oz) chopped walnuts**
**8 glacé cherries**

1 Place the apples in a saucepan with very little water and the honey. Cook gently, stirring, until the apples are pulped. Taste and add a little more honey to sweeten, if necessary.

2 Beat egg yolk into the apple and cook quickly, stirring, for 1 minute. Add the sultanas and leave until cold.

3 Whisk the egg white until stiff and standing in peaks. Fold in the sugar, then fold into the apple mixture.

4 Pile into a glass serving dish, sprinkle with the chopped walnuts and decorate with halved cherries.

5 Serve within 1 hour.

**35** **160**

## SUMMER PAVLOVA

*(Serves 6)*
450 g (1lb) strawberries
a little castor sugar for sprinkling
**PAVLOVA**
1 level teaspoon cornflour
1 level teaspoon vinegar
1 teaspoon vanilla essence
3 egg whites
200 g (7oz) castor sugar
**SHERRY CREAM SAUCE**
3 egg yolks
45 g (2½oz) castor sugar
3 tablespoons sweet sherry
150 ml (5fl oz) double cream

**1** Preheat a warm oven (150 deg C, 300 deg F, Gas 2), centre shelf. Cover a baking sheet with non-stick paper (or dampen and cover with greaseproof paper).
**2 To make the pavlova:** Mix together the cornflour, vinegar and vanilla essence.
**3** Whisk the egg whites until stiff and standing in peaks. Then gradually whisk in half the sugar to make a stiff, shiny meringue.
**4** Carefully fold in the remaining sugar and the cornflour mixture, using a metal spoon.
**5** Spread the mixture on the greaseproof paper to an even circle about 2.5 cm (1in) thick.
**6** Place in the oven and immediately reduce the heat to very cool (140 deg C, 275 deg F, Gas 1).
**7** Cook for 1 hour, when the pavlova should be crisp on the outside and marshmallow-like in the middle. Turn oven off and leave to cool in the oven without opening the door.
**8** Hull strawberries, halving if liked, and place in a basin. Sprinkle well with castor sugar.
**9 To prepare the sauce:** Place the egg yolks in a medium-sized bowl, add the sugar and sherry and stand over a saucepan of hot water.
**10** Whisk the mixture until thick and light and the whisk leaves a trail when lifted.
**11** Remove from heat and continue to whisk until mixture is cool. Place the bowl in ice-cold water and whisk occasionally until well chilled.
**12** Whisk the double cream until thick and fold into the egg mixture, then turn into a serving dish.
**13** Just before serving, place the pavlova on a serving plate. Spoon the strawberries into the centre. Serve the sherry cream sauce separately.

**30** **60**

## RASPBERRY CREAM GATEAU

*(Serves 6)*
125 g (4oz) soft margarine
125 g (4oz) castor sugar
2 large eggs
125 g (4oz) self-raising flour
1 level teaspoon baking powder
**FILLING**
125 g (4oz) frozen raspberries
50 g (2oz) soft margarine
125 g (4oz) icing sugar
¼ teaspoon vanilla essence
75 g (3oz) chopped almonds
3 level tablespoons redcurrant jelly
150 ml (5fl oz) double cream

**1** Preheat a warm oven (170 deg C, 325 deg F, Gas 3), shelf above centre: Lightly grease and flour a 20 cm (8in) square cake tin.
**2 To prepare the cake:** Place the margarine in a mixing bowl with the sugar and eggs.
**3** Sift in the flour and baking powder and beat the ingredients together for 2 minutes. Turn the mixture into the prepared tin, level surface with a knife.
**4** Bake for about 30 minutes, until springy to the touch. Remove from oven and allow to cool in tin for a few minutes, then turn out on to a wire rack to cool.
**5 To prepare the filling:** Meanwhile, allow the raspberries to thaw a little.
**6** Cream the margarine in a bowl, sieve in the icing sugar and beat well together until light and fluffy. Add the vanilla essence.
**7** Preheat a moderate grill, place the chopped almonds in the grill pan and grill until golden brown.
**8** Trim the edges of the cake and cut it in half horizontally.
**9** Spread some of the icing in the centre of the cake, sandwich together and spread the remainder of the icing over the sides.
**10** Press the browned nuts on to the sides of the cake. Arrange the raspberries on the surface of the cake leaving 1 cm (½in) around the edge.
**11** Gently melt the redcurrant jelly in a small saucepan. Cool slightly, and then spoon it over the raspberries on the cake.
**12** Whip the cream until softly stiff. Place in a piping bag fitted with a rosette nozzle and pipe a border of cream round the edge of the cake.

## COFFEE MERINGUE NESTS

*(Serves 6)*
**3 egg whites**
**150 g (6oz) castor sugar**
**50 g (2oz) butter**
**100 g (4oz) icing sugar**
**1 teaspoon coffee essence**
**150 ml (5fl oz) double cream**
**milk or plain chocolate vermicelli**
**small sugar Easter eggs (optional)**

**1** Preheat a very cool oven (110 deg C, 225 deg F, Gas ¼), shelves above and below centre. Line 2 baking sheets with non-stick paper or greaseproof paper. Draw six 7.5 cm (3in) circles on each. Oil the greaseproof paper.
**2** Whisk the egg whites until stiff and standing in peaks. Gradually add half the sugar, whisking well after each addition. Whisk until glossy, then fold in the remainder of the sugar.
**3** Divide the meringue between the 12 circles and spread it with a palette knife to fill the circles (or you can pipe the meringue into circles through a rosette nozzle).
**4** Place the two baking sheets in the oven—change their positions halfway through the cooking time. Cook for 1 hour, until the meringues are completey dried out. Remove the paper and cool on a wire tray.
**5** Cream together the butter and sieved icing sugar until light and fluffy. Add the coffee essence and mix well.
**6** Spread this mixture on half the meringue circles. Then cover with the remaining circles.
**7** Whip the cream until fairly stiff, place in a piping bag and pipe rosettes round the edge of each nest.
**8** Sprinkle the cream lightly with the chocolate vermicelli and decorate with the Easter eggs if liked.

## LEMONY FRUIT SALAD

*(Serves 6)*
**400 ml (¾ pint) water**
**75 g (3oz) castor sugar**
**1½ tablespoons lemon curd**
**3 apples**
**2 pears**
**2 oranges**
**125 g (4oz) black grapes, halved and de-seeded**
**125 g (4oz) green grapes, halved and de-seeded**
**2 bananas**

**1** Place the water and sugar in a saucepan and bring to the boil, stirring until the sugar has dissolved. Boil rapidly 3 minutes, then remove from heat and stir in the lemon curd. Leave to cool, then pour into a large bowl.
**2** Peel, quarter and core the apples and pears. Slice and add to the syrup.
**3** Cut the peel and pith away from the oranges using a very sharp knife, and cut the flesh across horizontally into slices. Halve these and add with the grapes to the fruit salad. Mix well and chill.
**4** Just before serving, peel and slice the bananas into the bowl. Mix well and serve with cream.

## ICE CREAM WITH CARAMEL RAISIN SAUCE

*(Serves 4)*
**4 portions vanilla ice cream**
**SAUCE**
**175 g (6oz) dark soft brown sugar**
**150 ml (¼ pint) cold water**
**25 g (1oz) butter or margarine**
**strip of lemon rind**
**15 g (½oz) cornflour**
**2 tablespoons water**
**40 g (1½oz) raisins**
**1 teaspoon lemon juice**

**1 To make the sauce:** Place the sugar and water in a small saucepan. Heat gently until the sugar has dissolved, stirring occasionally.
**2** Add the butter or margarine and lemon rind and boil rapidly for 3 minutes.
**3** Blend the cornflour with the cold water until smooth.
**4** Stir in a little of the hot liquid and then pour the cornflour mixture into the pan, stirring continuously. Bring to the boil, stirring, and simmer for 2 minutes.
**5** Remove the lemon rind and add the raisins and lemon juice. Taste and add a little more lemon juice if liked.
**6** Leave to cool in a small bowl or serve hot.
**7** Arrange the ice cream on individual dishes and then spoon the sauce over it. Serve immediately.

## CHOCOLATE BANANA BOATS

*(Serves 4)*
125 g (4oz) plain chocolate
150 ml (¼ pint) hot water
2 level tablespoons castor sugar
50 g (2oz) butter
4 frozen chocolate éclairs, thawed
4 bananas
3 level tablespoons chopped nuts

1 Break the chocolate into pieces and place in a medium-sized saucepan. Add the hot water and sugar to the chocolate and heat gently to melt.
2 When the chocolate and sugar have dissolved bring to the boil and allow to simmer slowly until the sauce has reduced and is fairly syrupy. Remove from the heat, add the butter and stir in until melted. Allow the sauce to cool slightly.
3 Cut the éclairs in half lengthways and arrange in pairs on individual plates with the cream side uppermost.
4 Peel the bananas and cut each one in half lengthways. Place a banana half on each éclair and spoon a little chocolate sauce over the bananas.
5 Sprinkle with the chopped nuts and serve.

## BAKED CUSTARD WITH SPICED ORANGES

*(Serves 4)*
4 eggs
40 g (1½oz) castor sugar
1 teaspoon vanilla essence
550 ml (1 pint) milk
SPICED ORANGES
3 large oranges
½ level teaspoon powdered cinnamon
1 level teaspoon castor sugar

1 Preheat a warm oven (170 deg C, 325 deg F, Gas 3), centre shelf.
2 Whisk eggs in a basin with the sugar and vanilla.
3 Heat milk almost to boiling point and stir in the eggs.
4 Strain the mixture into a litre (2 pint) ovenproof dish. Half fill a baking tin with cold water and place the dish of custard in it. This prevents custard from over-cooking.
5 Bake in the oven for 70 minutes, or until set. Remove from the tin of water and leave to cool.

6 **To make the spiced oranges:** Cut the pith and peel away from the oranges with a very sharp knife. Cut out the segments between the membranes.
7 Mix together the cinnamon and sugar.
8 Just before serving, arrange the orange segments over the custard and sprinkle with the cinnamon sugar.

## PEAR AND CREAM CHEESE DELIGHT

*(Serves 3)*
425 g (15oz) can pear halves
125 g (4oz) soft cream cheese
25 g (1oz) walnuts, finely chopped
2 level tablespoons strawberry jam
2 teaspoons lemon juice
1 level teaspoon arrowroot

1 Drain the pears, reserving the juice. Dry the pear halves on kitchen paper.
2 Put the cream cheese in a small bowl and blend with 1 tablespoon of the pear juice and the walnuts.
3 Divide the cream cheese mixture between 3 pear halves. Place a corresponding pear half on each to make three whole pears, and then place them in individual serving dishes.
4 Melt the jam in a small saucepan with the lemon juice. Then sieve the mixture, rinse the saucepan, and return the mixture to the pan.
5 Blend the arrowroot with a little water and add to the sieved jam. Cook slowly, stirring continuously, until the mixture thickens and clear—about 2 minutes.
6 Pour the sauce over the pears and serve.

## QUICK CHOCOLATE MOUSSE

*(Serves 3)*
50 g (2oz) plain chocolate
2 large eggs, separated
a few drops of vanilla essence or rum

1 Break the chocolate into small pieces and put in a small bowl over a saucepan of hot but not boiling water. Allow to melt and remove from the heat.
2 Add the egg yolks to the melted chocolate and beat well for 3 minutes until the mixture thickens. Add the vanilla essence or rum.
3 Whisk the egg whites until very stiff. Fold the egg whites into the chocolate mixture until well mixed.
4 Turn into small glasses and chill to set.

# CHOCOLATE STRAWBERRY CASTLES

*(Serves 4)*
550 ml (1 pint) packet strawberry blancmange
2 heaped tablespoons sugar
550 ml (1 pint) milk
2 large firm bananas
CHOCOLATE SAUCE
3 level tablespoons chocolate spread
1 tablespoon top milk

**1** Blend blancmange powder and sugar in a basin with 3 tablespoons of the milk.
**2** Bring the remaining milk to the boil and stir into the basin. Return the mixture to the pan and simmer gently for 2 minutes, stirring continuously.
**3** Pour into 4 teacups, or into 150 ml (¼ pint) cream or yogurt cartons, rinsed out with cold water.
**4** Chill for at least 2 hours until set.
**5 To make the chocolate sauce:** Spoon the chocolate spread into a basin and stir in the top milk.
**6** To serve, turn out the blancmange on to individual plates or a large serving dish. Arrange half a sliced banana round each one and top with a generous spoonful of the chocolate sauce.

# CHERRY AND ALMOND CREAM FLAN

*(Serves 4-6)*
1 baked pastry flan case, about
   15-18 cm (6-7in) wide
4 level tablespoons black cherry jam
150 ml (5fl oz) double cream
1 egg white
a few drops of almond essence
3 macaroons

**1** Place the pastry flan case on a serving plate. Spread the cherry jam over the base of the flan.
**2** Whisk the double cream until softly stiff.
**3** Whisk the egg white, with a clean whisk, until stiff and standing in peaks. Add a few drops of almond essence.
**4** Crumble the macaroons into a bowl and fold in the double cream and egg white.
**5** Spoon this mixture over the cherry jam and serve immediately while the macaroons are still crisp and give texture to the topping.

# SPICY PEAR FLAN

*(Serves 4-6)*
225 g (8oz) ginger nut biscuits
50 g (2oz) butter
1 rounded tablespoon golden syrup
425 g (15oz) can pear halves
2 level tablespoons custard powder
¼ level teaspoon cinnamon
glacé cherries to decorate

**1** Place the biscuits in a bowl or between 2 large sheets of greaseproof paper. Crush finely with a rolling pin.
**2** Heat the butter and syrup in a small saucepan until melted. Add the biscuit crumbs and mix well.
**3** Press into a 23 cm (9in) pie plate and chill while preparing filling.
**4** Drain the pears and make the juice up to 250 ml (½ pint) with water.
**5** Place the custard powder and cinnamon in a saucepan and slowly blend in the pear juice. Bring to the boil, stirring continuously. Simmer for 2 minutes to thicken, then remove from heat and allow to cool slightly.
**6** Arrange the pears in the flan case with cut sides down. Spoon the sauce over the pears and leave to set. Then decorate with a few glacé cherries.

# NO-BAKE GOSSAMER PIE

*(Serves 6)*
175 g (6oz) ginger biscuits
75 g (3oz) butter
225 g (9oz) carton frozen lemon
   mousse, thawed
225 g (9oz) carton frozen strawberry
   or chocolate mousse, thawed
chocolate vermicelli

**1** Butter a 23 cm (9in) plate or shallow dish.
**2** Place the biscuits in a bowl or between 2 large sheets of greaseproof paper. Crush finely with a rolling pin.
**3** Melt the butter in a saucepan and stir in the biscuit crumbs. Press the crumbs onto the prepared dish to form a crunchy base. Leave for at least 1 hour until set.
**4** Open both cartons of mousse and, using a different spoon for each flavour, arrange alternate spoonfuls slightly overlapping on the biscuit base.
**5** Sprinkle with chocolate vermicelli and serve at once.

## GRAPE AND APPLE RING

*(Serves 4)*
**350 g (12oz) cooking apples, peeled, cored
  and sliced**
**50 g (2oz) granulated sugar**
**150 ml (¼ pint) apple juice**
**1 packet lime-flavoured jelly**
**75 ml (3fl oz) water**
**175 g (6oz) black and green grapes**
**4 thin lemon slices to garnish**

1 Put the apples, sugar and apple juice into a saucepan and simmer gently until soft—about 10 minutes.
2 Meanwhile heat the jelly in the water, and stir until dissolved.
3 When the apples are soft, place in a bowl with the liquid jelly. Stand the bowl in ice-cold water and whisk the ingredients together with a rotary beater until cool and foamy.
4 Wet a 550 ml (1 pint) ring mould and pour in the apple jelly mixture. Chill until set.
5 Meanwhile halve and de-seed the grapes.
6 When the jelly has set carefully turn it out on to a plate. Fill the centre with grapes and arrange some round the edge. Decorate the ring with lemon slices.

## CHILLED MELON FAILAND

*(Serves 4)*
**juice of 2 large oranges and shredded rind ½ orange**
**100 g (4oz) granulated sugar**
**1 ripe melon**

1 Make up the orange juice to 225 ml (8fl oz) with water. Pour into a small saucepan, add the orange rind and half the sugar and heat gently, stirring, until the sugar dissolves. Bring to the boil and simmer for 5 minutes.
2 Meanwhile remove the rind and seeds from melon and cut into 2 cm (1in) cubes; place in a bowl. Pour the hot orange syrup over, cover and leave until cold. Chill well for several hours, or overnight, before serving.
3 Meanwhile have ready a piece of oiled greaseproof paper on a tin. Place the remaining sugar in a small saucepan and add 1 tablespoon water. Heat gently, stirring, until the sugar dissolves, then bring to boil and boil rapidly until golden brown. Pour on to the oiled paper.
4 Leave until hard, then crush into small pieces. Sprinkle over the melon just before serving.

## BLACKCURRANT
## MERINGUE FLAN

*(Serves 5-6)*
**75 g (3oz) butter, melted**
**225 g (8oz) digestive biscuits, crushed**
**175 g (6oz) blackcurrants**
**150 ml (¼ pint) water**
**1 level tablespoon cornflour**
**2 level tablespoons sugar**
**150 ml (¼ pint) double cream**
**10 baby meringues**

1 Mix together the melted butter and biscuit crumbs, and press over base and up sides of 23 cm (9in) fluted flan dish or ring set on a baking sheet. Chill until set.
2 Meanwhile place blackcurrants and the measured water in a small saucepan, bring to boil and simmer for 2 to 3 minutes until tender. Pour through a sieve and return the syrup to the saucepan, reserving fruit.
3 Blend the cornflour and sugar with a little cold water until smooth. Stir into the syrup and bring to the boil, stirring constantly. Remove from heat and stir in the reserved fruit. Leave until cool.
4 Whisk the cream until thick. Then spoon into the flan case with the blackcurrant mixture and meringues.
5 Keep chilled until ready to serve.

## RASPBERRY CONDÉ

*(Serves 4)*
**225 g (8oz) raspberries, fresh or frozen**
**1 tablespoon water**
**1 rounded tablespoon castor sugar**
**2 level teaspoons gelatine**
**440 g (15½oz) can creamed rice pudding**
**150 ml (¼ pint) double cream**

1 Put half the raspberries in a bowl, sprinkle with the sugar and leave for about 3 hours to soften.
2 Place the water in a cup and sprinkle with the gelatine. Stand the cup in a pan of hot water until the gelatine dissolves. Stir into the creamed rice pudding.
3 Whisk the cream until fairly thick and fold into the rice pudding. Divide between 4 glasses and arrange the remaining raspberries on top.
4 Rub the sugared raspberries through a sieve and spoon the purée over the raspberries and rice.
5 Chill well before serving.

**Continental Cake,** see opposite

# CAKES & BISCUITS

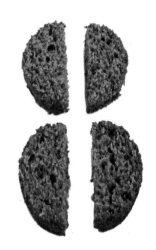

*The well-filled cake tin or biscuit jar is a family favourite—these recipes help you find the time to make those popular extras. The clocks do not show time needed for cooling unless the recipes give instructions for icing or decorating, which must be done when the bakes are cool*

**30**  **155**

## CONTINENTAL CAKE

*(Makes 10 slices)*
275 g (10oz) plain flour
½ level teaspoon salt
75 g (3oz) butter or margarine
25 g (1oz) fresh yeast, or 1 level tablespoon dried
    yeast plus ½ level teaspoon sugar
5 tablespoons milk
50 g (2oz) castor sugar
175 g (6oz) mixed dried fruit
grated rind and juice of 1 lemon
½ level teaspoon cinnamon
2 large eggs, beaten
TOPPING
25 g (1oz) butter
40 g (1½oz) plain flour
25 g (1oz) soft brown sugar
½ level teaspoon cinnamon
2 tablespoons marmalade or apricot jam

**1** Sift the flour and salt into a mixing bowl and rub in the butter or margarine until the mixture resembles fine breadcrumbs.
**2** Rub in the fresh yeast. If using dried yeast, warm the milk, dissolve the sugar in it and sprinkle the dried yeast on top. Leave mixture to become frothy—about 10 minutes.
**3** Mix in the sugar, dried fruit, lemon rind and cinnamon.
**4** Add the eggs with the milk, or milk and dried yeast, and stir with a wooden spoon, to make a very soft dough.

**5** Well grease a 1½ litre (2½ pint) loaf tin and spread in the dough.
**6 To make the topping:** Rub the butter into the flour, add the soft brown sugar and cinnamon.
**7** Spread the marmalade or apricot jam lightly over the top of the cake and sprinkle the mixture over.
**8** Cover the tin with a lightly oiled polythene bag and leave in a warm place, or at room temperature, until doubled in size. This may take 1-2 hours.
**9** Meanwhile preheat a moderately hot oven (200 deg C, 400 deg F, Gas 6), centre shelf.
**10** Bake the cake for 35-40 minutes until well risen—if topping starts to burn, cover with greaseproof paper.
**11** Cool in tin for 10 minutes, then turn on to a rack.
**12** Served sliced and spread with butter.

*See picture opposite*

**15**  **120**

## FAMILY FRUIT CAKE

*(Makes 12 slices)*
225 g (8oz) butter or margarine
225 g (8oz) icing sugar
250 g (9oz) plain flour
½ level teaspoon baking powder
4 eggs, beaten
grated rind and juice of 1 lemon
125 g (4oz) walnuts, chopped
225 g (8oz) sultanas
225 g (8oz) chopped mixed peel

**1** Preheat a cool oven (150 deg C, 300 deg F, Gas 2), centre shelf. Line and grease a deep 20 cm (8in) cake tin.

**2** Cream together the butter or margarine and sieved icing sugar in a mixing bowl until light and fluffy.

**3** Sieve the flour and baking powder into the mixture and stir in with the eggs. Add the lemon rind and juice, walnuts, sultanas and mixed peel. Mix well.

**4** Transfer the mixture to the prepared tin and spread evenly, making a small well in the centre.

**5** Bake for about 2 hours—until a skewer inserted into the centre comes out clean.

**6** Cool in the tin for 30 minutes. Then remove from tin, tear off the lining paper and cool on a wire rack.

## CREAMY CURD SPONGE

*(Serves 4-6)*
**125 g (4oz) butter or margarine**
**125 g (4oz) castor sugar**
**2 large eggs, beaten**
**grated rind and juice of 1 lemon**
**125 g (4oz) self-raising flour**
**FILLING**
**75 g (3oz) cream cheese**
**2 level tablespoons lemon curd**
**125 g (4oz) icing sugar**
**angelica to decorate**

**1** Preheat a moderately hot oven (190 deg C, 375 deg F, Gas 5), centre shelf. Lightly grease and flour two 18 cm (7in) sandwich tins.

**2** Cream together the butter or margarine and sugar in a mixing bowl until the mixture is light and fluffy.

**3** Gradually beat the eggs into the creamed mixture with the lemon rind, beating well after each addition. Sift the flour and fold into the mixture, then stir in the lemon juice.

**4** Divide between the 2 prepared tins; level the surface with a knife.

**5** Bake for about 25 minutes, until springy to the touch. Remove from the oven and leave for 5 minutes before removing from tin. Then cool on a wire rack.

**6 To make the filling:** Place the cream cheese in a small bowl, add the lemon curd and beat together. Sieve the icing sugar and beat into the mixture.

**7** Sandwich the cakes together with half the filling and spread the remainder on top, swirling it into an attractive pattern. Cut the angelica into large diamond-shaped leaves and use to decorate the edge.

## CHERRY ORANGE LOAF

*(Makes 10 slices)*
**350 g (12oz) self-raising flour**
**½ level teaspoon salt**
**75 g (3oz) castor sugar**
**50 g (2oz) glacé cherries, chopped**
**225 g (8oz) dried mixed fruit and chopped peel**
**grated rind of 1 orange**
**50 g (2oz) butter or margarine**
**2 eggs, beaten**
**8-9 tablespoons milk**
**DECORATION**
**125 g (4oz) icing sugar**
**juice 1 orange**
**25 g (1oz) glacé cherries**
**crystallised orange slices**

**1** Preheat a warm oven (170 deg C, 325 deg F, Gas 3), centre shelf. Grease and line the base of a 1½ litre (2½ pint) loaf tin.

**2** Sift the flour and salt into a mixing bowl and add the sugar, glacé cherries, dried fruit and peel, and orange rind. Mix well.

**3** Melt the butter in a small saucepan.

**4** Mix the eggs milk and butter together and pour gradually into the dry mixture, stirring. Mix well until evenly blended.

**5** Turn into the prepared loaf tin, level the surface, and bake for 1¼-1½ hours until a skewer inserted into the centre comes out clean.

**6** Turn out and cool on a wire rack.

**7 To decorate:** Sift the icing sugar into a small bowl and beat in enough of the orange juice to make a thin coating consistency.

**8** Spread over the top of the loaf and allow to trickle down the sides. Decorate with glacé cherry halves and crystallised orange slices.

## RAISIN CREAM CHEESE RING

*(Serves 4-6)*
**225 g (8oz) self-raising flour**
**pinch salt**
**50 g (2oz) butter**
**75 g (3oz) seedless raisins**
**2 level teaspoons castor sugar**
**150 ml (¼ pint) milk**
**extra milk for brushing**
**50 g (2oz) cream cheese**
**paprika**

1 Preheat a hot oven (220 deg C, 425 deg F, Gas 7), shelf towards top. Grease a large flat baking sheet.
2 Place the flour and salt in a bowl. Rub in the butter until the mixture resembles fine breadcrumbs. Stir in the raisins and sugar. Make a well in the mixture and pour in all the milk. Mix to a soft dough, using a fork.
3 Turn the dough on to a well-floured surface and knead lightly into a ball.
4 Roll out to about 1.5 cm (½in) thickness and cut into rounds with a 5 cm (2in) pastry cutter. Roll the remaining pieces together and cut into rounds.
5 Arrange the scones slightly overlapping in a circle or oval on the baking sheet. Brush the top lightly with milk to glaze.
6 Bake for 12 minutes, until they are well risen.
7 To serve hot, remove scone circle intact on to a serving dish (or cool on a wire rack).
8 To serve: Beat the cream cheese until smooth, turn into a small dish and sprinkle with paprika. Place the dish in the centre of the scone ring.
9 Break off portions of scone and spread them with the cream cheese.

## SANDWICH ANTOINETTE

*(Makes 6-8 slices)*
**65 g (2½oz) butter or margarine**
**3 large eggs**
**75 g (3oz) castor sugar**
**65 g (2½oz) plain flour**
**2-3 tablespoons black cherry jam**
**icing sugar for sifting**
**CUSTARD CREAM**
**1 egg yolk**
**25 g (1oz) castor sugar**
**25 g (1oz) plain flour**
**½ teaspoon vanilla essence**
**150 ml (¼ pint) milk**
**2 tablespoons single cream**
**icing sugar to decorate**

1 Preheat a moderately hot oven (190 deg C, 375 deg F, Gas 5), centre shelf. Line the base of two 18 cm (7in) sandwich tins with greaseproof paper and thoroughly grease base and sides.
2 Melt the butter or margarine and leave to cool.
3 Break the eggs into a mixing bowl, add the sugar and whisk over a pan of hot, but not boiling, water until the mixture is thick and pale. The whisk should leave a trail when lifted.
4 Sift in the flour and fold in gently using a metal spoon. Then strain in the cooled butter or margarine and carefully fold it in.
5 Pour into the prepared sandwich tins and bake about 25 minutes. Turn out on to a wire rack to cool, removing the greaseproof papers.
6 To make the custard cream: Meanwhile beat egg yolk and sugar together in a basin until thick and creamy.

Stir in the flour and vanilla essence. Heat the milk and stir into the mixture. Pour into a small saucepan and bring to the boil, stirring continuously. Cook gently for 3 minutes. Cool slightly and beat in the cream. Turn into a basin and leave until cold.
7 Place one cake on a plate, spread with jam and then custard cream. Place the other cake on top. Sift a little icing sugar over.

## CHOCOLATE COOKIE CAKE

*(Makes 6 slices)*
**175 g (6oz) plain chocolate**
**25 g (1oz) butter**
**225 g (8oz) semi-sweet biscuits, crushed**
**50 g (2oz) glacé cherries, quartered**
**25 g (1oz) blanched almonds, chopped**
**1 level teaspoon vanilla essence**

1 Break the chocolate into pieces and put in a medium-sized bowl. Place over a pan of hot water to melt.
2 Remove the basin of chocolate from the pan and add the butter. Allow it to melt then stir in the crushed biscuits, cherries, almonds and vanilla essence. Mix well.
3 Line a 450 g (1lb) loaf tin with foil. Press in the mixture and chill in refrigerator for 2 hours until firm.
4 Turn out on to a serving dish and cut into slices.

## OATIE PEANUT CRUNCH

*(Makes 8 pieces)*
55 g (2½oz) butter
1 slightly rounded tablespoon golden syrup
50 g (2oz) demerara sugar
1 level tablespoon peanut butter
125 g (4oz) rolled oats
25 g (1oz) salted peanuts

**1** Preheat a moderate oven (180 deg C, 350 deg F, Gas 4), centre shelf. Grease an 18 cm (7in) round sandwich tin.
**2** Heat the butter, syrup and sugar gently in a medium-sized saucepan, stirring with a wooden spoon until butter has melted. Remove from the heat and stir in the peanut butter and rolled oats.
**3** Press mixture into the prepared tin, using the back of a wet wooden spoon. Chop the peanuts coarsely and press over the mixture, or leave in halves and press in lightly round the edge.
**4** Bake for 20-25 minutes. Then while still hot mark deeply with a knife into 8 wedges. Leave to cool in the tin before cutting through.

## APPLE AND CINNAMON ROCKIES

*(Makes 12)*
175 g (6oz) self-raising flour
1 level teaspoon ground cinnamon
75 g (3oz) granulated sugar
75 g (3oz) butter or margarine
1 large egg, beaten
175 g (6oz) cooking apple, peeled, cored and chopped

**1** Preheat a moderately hot oven (200 deg C, 400 deg F, Gas 6), shelf above centre. Grease a baking sheet.
**2** Place the flour, cinnamon and sugar in a bowl. Rub in the butter or margarine until the mixture resembles fine breadcrumbs. Mix to a stiff paste with the beaten egg and stir in the chopped apple.
**3** Flour the hands lightly and pinch the mixture into 12 evenly sized heaps. Place on the prepared baking sheet.
**4** Bake for about 20 minutes until golden brown and firm to the touch. Cool on a wire rack.

## BASIC BISCUIT MIX

*(Makes 16 biscuits)*
150 g (5oz) plain flour
75 g (3oz) butter
50 g (2oz) castor sugar
½ a lightly beaten egg

**1** Preheat a moderate oven (180 deg C, 350 deg F, Gas 4), shelf above centre. Lightly grease and sprinkle flour on a baking sheet.
**2** Sieve the flour into a large bowl. Add the butter and sugar and the egg.
**3** Using fingertips, knead the mixture together until it forms one piece.
**4** Roll out on a floured surface to a ½ cm (¼in) thickness.
**5** Using a 7 cm (2½in) fluted or plain cutter cut out twelve rounds. Press and knead the trimmings together. Roll out and cut 4 more rounds.
**6** Place the rounds on the baking sheet and prick lightly with a fork.
**7** Bake for 12-15 minutes until lightly browned. Cool on a wire rack.
**Note:** To vary the basic mix, grated lemon or orange rind, mixed spices, grated nutmeg, or cinnamon may be added in stage 2.

## TOASTED COCONUT ROUNDS

*(Makes 16 biscuits)*
1 quantity of basic biscuit mix (recipe above)
1 egg white
3 level tablespoons desiccated coconut
4 glacé cherries, quartered

**1** Follow Basic Biscuit Mix recipe to the end of stage 6.
**2** Brush the rounds with egg white. Sprinkle on the coconut and press it in lightly. Place a quartered cherry in the centre of each biscuit.
**3** Bake for 12-15 minutes. Cool on a wire rack.

## HONEYED FLORENTINES

*(Makes 16 biscuits)*
**15 g (½oz) butter**
**1 level tablespoon honey**
**50 g (2oz) glacé cherries, chopped**
**25 g (1oz) blanched almonds, chopped**
**1 quantity of basic biscuit mix (recipe opposite)**
**75 g (3oz) plain chocolate**

**1** Melt the butter with the honey in a small saucepan and bring them to the boil. Then remove from heat.
**2** Add the cherries and nuts and mix well. Allow to cool.
**3** Follow Basic Biscuit Mix recipe to the end of stage 6.
**4** Place a small amount of the cherry and nut topping in the centre of each round.
**5** Bake for 12-15 minutes. Cool on a wire tray.
**6** Melt the chocolate in a small bowl over a pan of hot, not boiling, water.
**7** Roll the edge of each biscuit in the chocolate and place on waxed or greaseproof paper to harden.

## ICED GINGER FINGERS

*(Makes 20 biscuits)*
**1 quantity of basic biscuit mix (recipe on page 90)**
**150 g (5oz) icing sugar**
**1 tablespoon warm water**
**50 g (2oz) stem ginger**

**1** Follow Basic Biscuit Mix recipe to the end of stage 3.
**4** Roll out the mixture on a lightly floured surface and cut into 20 fingers 7 by 4 cm (2½ by 1½in).
**5** Place fingers on the prepared baking sheet and prick lightly with a fork. Bake for 12-15 minutes until lightly browned. Cool on a wire rack.
**6** Sieve the sugar into a medium-sized bowl and gradually beat in the water until the icing is smooth.
**7** Drain the ginger from the syrup and chop fairly finely.
**8** Spoon a little of the icing along the centre of the biscuits and sprinkle with the chopped ginger.

## ALMOND MERINGUE CRISPS

*(Makes 16 biscuits)*
**25 g (1oz) blanched almonds**
**1 quantity of basic biscuit mix (recipe opposite)**
**1 egg white**
**50 g (2oz) castor sugar**

**1** Chop the almonds finely, and lightly brown under the grill or in a small, heavy frying pan. Allow to cool.
**2** Follow Basic Biscuit Mix recipe to the end of stage 6.
**3** Whisk egg white till stiff and standing in peaks. Fold in the sugar and cooled nuts.
**4** Spread the meringue over the biscuits, leaving a small rim round the edge. Bake for 12-15 minutes until golden brown. Cool on a wire tray.

# Index